Creative
WALL
DECORATING

Cover pictures: (1) Elizabeth Whiting &
Associates/Brian Harrison; (tr) Homes &
Gardens/Robert Harding Syndication; (br)
Eaglemoss/Steve Tanner.

Page 1: Abode UK; Page 3: Country Homes &
Interiors/Robert Harding Syndication; Page 4:
Eaglemoss Publications/Steve Tanner; Page 5: Woman
& Home/PWA International.

First published in the USA in 1996
by Betterway Books,
an imprint of F&W Publications Inc.,
1507 Dana Avenue,
Cincinnati, Ohio 45207.

ISBN 1-55870-415-9

Manufactured in Hong Kong

10 9 8 7 6 5 4 3 2

Creative WALL DECORATING

BETTERWAY BOOKS

Contents

SPONGE PAINTING

*The soft, mottled pattern produced by sponging a
second layer of paint over a base coat adds a stylish broken colour effect to
the walls of a room and decorative interest to accessories.*

S ponging is an easy, instant paint effect that gives a pleasing, mottled appearance to a surface. As the name implies, the technique involves using a sponge to apply one or more colours to a solid base colour. The final look will depend on the number of coats of paint sponged on – the more there are, the denser the effect – and, most importantly, the colours used. With two close shades of the one colour, the effect is very subtle – from a distance the colours will merge yet not look as flat as an area painted in one colour. If two, or even three, quite different colours are layered the effect is more dramatic.

Because it is such a simple, quick technique, sponging is ideal for covering large expanses of wall, but it also works well on smaller surfaces such as a blanket box, a wall panel or a cupboard door. A more practical advantage of the technique is that it helps disguise obtrusive pipes and radiators. Experiment with different sponge effects on scrap paper before you start work – the following pages show you the basic techniques and there are suggestions for small creative projects.

As well as adding overall interest to a plain expanse of wall, sponging can be used for dramatic creative effects. This bold scheme is made even richer with panels of gold sponged over the red base coat.

SPONGING TECHNIQUE

Emulsion (latex) is the best choice for sponging walls – it is low odour, fairly inexpensive and easy to use, and the base coat can be applied with a roller. In general, two or more sponged colours give a more pleasing effect than one – using just one colour can sometimes look spotty unless the sponged colour is closely related to the base coat. Always try out various colourways on paper before starting work on a project – hold the paper samples up to the wall to test the result.

The sponge you use also affects the final look. Natural sea sponges are best; they are expensive but they produce a wonderfully varied pattern which isn't possible to imitate using a synthetic sponge. However, synthetic sponges are cheaper and more readily available. If you use a synthetic sponge, tear it into an irregular shape and apply the paint with the inner surface.

For a particularly subtle effect, you can dilute the sponging paint with water – test this out on your sample. And if you apply too much paint, remedy the effect by lifting off some of the excess with a dry sponge.

SPONGING ON WALLS

YOU WILL NEED

❖ EMULSION (LATEX) PAINTS
❖ ROLLER
❖ ROLLER TRAY
❖ RUBBER GLOVES
❖ SPONGE
❖ LINING or SCRAP PAPER

1 Testing the result To make sure that the colours you have chosen work well together, first test the effect on a piece of scrap paper or wallpaper lining paper.

2 Painting the base coat Check that the walls are sound and well prepared. Apply one coat of paint with a roller and allow to dry. If the colour underneath was dark, you may need to paint on another base coat and allow to dry. Clean the roller tray thoroughly.

3 Loading the sponge Condition a new sponge by soaking it in water, then wringing it out. Pour some of the second colour into the tray and dip the sponge lightly into it. To achieve the right soft speckled mark, and avoid paint runs, don't allow the sponge to soak up too much paint – it should be almost dry. Blot off any excess on scrap paper or the ridged surface of the tray.

4 Sponging on colour Working from the top of the wall, dab the sponge lightly over the surface. Turn the sponge as you work to vary the pattern. If you are sponging with just one colour, keep the marks as close together as possible for an overall, even effect. If you are using two or more colours you can space them out a little more. Avoid overlaps, especially at corners and beside doors or windows where paint can build up.

5 Adding another colour (optional) Rinse out the sponge thoroughly. Wait for the paint to dry, then apply the second sponged coat over the first, filling in any gaps between the first colour yet still allowing some of the base colour to show through.

◀ *Three different shades of soft deep yellow, shown below, were used for the broken paint effect on this stylish wall. For an extra impression of depth, two colours were sponged over the base coat – if you don't want a build-up of colour, one colour sponged over the base coat may be enough.*

T I P

SPONGING AWKWARD AREAS

When sponging narrow areas such as door or window frames, avoid getting paint on the surrounding area by using a sponging off technique. Use a brush, not a sponge, to apply the second colour over the base coat. Then dab a clean sponge over the wet paint to remove some of the colour.

SPONGING TILES

Sponging ceramic tiles is a simple way to give a fresh look to a bathroom or kitchen wall, or to disguise unattractive tiling. The finish described below is hardwearing enough for most bathroom or kitchen tiles, but is not suitable for the tiling around a shower or any other area that will be constantly damp. In this bathroom one colour was sponged over plain white tiles, and a second was sponged on top in a diagonal pattern using a square cut out of card as a template.

It is important to clean the tiles and the grouting thoroughly and leave them to dry out before you apply the paint. Use a solvent/oil-based eggshell paint for sponging over tiles – it has good covering power, and does not need an undercoat. If you are sponging over patterned tiles, or you want a base colour that's different from the original colour of the tiles, prepare the surface as described below then cover the tiles with a base coat of solvent/oil-based gloss or eggshell. Work in a ventilated room when applying solvent-based paints; clean all equipment with white (mineral) spirit.

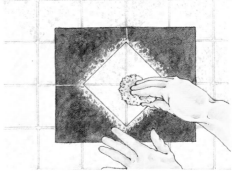

YOU WILL NEED

- ❖ METHYLATED SPIRIT/ DENATURED ALCOHOL
- ❖ SOFT CLOTHS
- ❖ SOLVENT/OIL-BASED EGGSHELL PAINT
- ❖ ROLLER TRAY
- ❖ SPONGE
- ❖ SCRAP PAPER
- ❖ WHITE (MINERAL) SPIRIT
- ❖ CARDBOARD
- ❖ RULER AND PENCIL
- ❖ CRAFT KNIFE

These bathroom tiles have a new look with a stylish diamond pattern.

1 Cleaning the surface Wash the tiles down thoroughly with soap and water and leave for at least 24 hours to dry.

2 Preparing for painting To remove any residue of grease and evaporate all remaining moisture off the surface, wipe over the tiles carefully with a little methylated spirit (denatured alcohol) applied to a soft cloth, paying particular attention to the grouting.

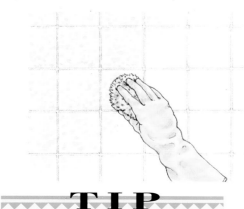

3 Sponging Pour a little paint into the tray, and spread out to a thin layer. Dab the sponge into the paint; remove any excess and test the effect on scrap paper. Carefully dab on over the tiles. Leave the paint to dry but clean out tray and sponge at once.

TIP

SPONGED BORDER
As a small first-time sponging project, experiment with a sponged border to add interest to plain tiles. Using the same sponge technique as above, cut out a shape from card, and sponge directly through it on to the tiles.

4 Sponging diagonals Using a craft knife, cut out a square from the card, with the sides equal to the tile diagonal – the square will provide a template for the sponged diamond shapes. For accurate positioning, mark the continuation of the grout lines on the card. Sponge colour through the square template – if necessary, avoid smudging by sponging alternate diamonds .

COLOURWASHING

The subtle blending of translucent washes of colour gives walls an appealingly soft and weathered character which is traditionally associated with a natural country style.

Created by quickly applying one or two thin washes of colour over a base coat, colourwashing is suitable for rooms of all shapes and sizes. A rich depth can be achieved with deep colours, while soft colourwashing provides an ideal background for wallpaper borders and other decorating techniques such as stencilling and block printing.

One of the main advantages of colourwashing is that it's really easy to get a pleasing result. All you need is emulsion (latex) paint, brushes and water. The technique is ideal for walls that are uneven or in poor condition, as any imperfections merge in to become part of the finish. And if you are dissatisfied with the colour of a newly painted wall, a colourwash technique is quicker and uses less paint than painting the wall again in the ordinary way. All that you need do is cover the painted wall with a thinned wash of a coordinating or contrasting colour.

A wash of yellow over a white base coat brings a hint of sunshine into a room.

COLOURWASHING A WALL

To colourwash walls, a thin wash of diluted paint, normally emulsion (latex), is brushed in all directions over a base coat of dried paint.

For the wash you can use a colour that tones or contrasts with the base coat, depending on the effect you want to achieve. Generally, colourwashing works best where the wash is a slightly darker shade than the base coat.

The colourwashing technique is very simple. When brushing on the colourwash, you need to apply enough pressure to leave brush marks that show up clearly. A dry brush is then lightly stroked over the wet paint to soften and blur the original brush marks and reveal the background colour. The more you brush out the wet paint, the more subtle the colourwash will be.

One wash of colour over the base coat is usually enough to achieve the right effect, but for greater depth you can build up the colour by using two different coloured washes. To do this, brush out and soften the first wash while it's still wet, then allow it to dry completely before applying the next. Don't attempt to use more than two colourwashes over the base coat, or you're likely to lose the lovely translucence of the wash.

Before you start painting a wall, it's a good idea to buy some tester pots of paint and experiment with different colour mixes on a large sheet of lining paper. Stick the paper on the wall with masking tape to check the result in both day and artificial light.

It's also sensible to wear old clothes when you're colourwashing – it can be a messy business.

CHOOSING COLOURS

Soft pale colours have a carefree, country cottage feel and usually look best applied over a white background. In a cool sunless room, create a sun-dappled effect by using bright yellow, coral or pink. Try cool tones of aqua, moss green or hydrangea blue in a warm sunny room.

Dark colours produce strong, sophisticated effects, but as the paint is applied thinly the colour is unlikely to be overpowering. Try a pastel base with two rich colours over it. Be bold with your choice of colours – paint a pale pink wall with magenta, for example, and add a scarlet wash, or experiment with emerald green over turquoise.

> ### YOU WILL NEED
> - ❖ PLASTIC SHEETS or NEWSPAPER
> - ❖ ROLLER for the base coat
> - ❖ TWO PAINT BRUSHES each 100-150mm (4-6in) wide
> - ❖ VINYL MATT EMULSION (FLAT LATEX) in a base colour and one or two colours for the wash
> - ❖ WATER for thinning paint
> - ❖ PAINT KETTLE
> - ❖ COTTON RAG

1 Applying the base colour Protect the floor and nearby furniture with plastic sheets or newspaper, then use a roller or paint brush to paint the walls with a matt emulsion base coat. Allow to dry and add a second coat of the same colour. Leave to dry overnight.

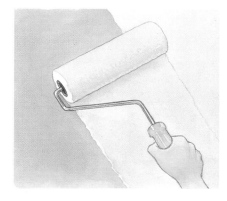

2 Mixing the wash To thin the colourwash emulsion so that the colour beneath shows through, dilute one part paint to four parts water in the paint kettle.

3 Applying the wash Dip the brush into the wash and remove excess with a rag. Working quickly on a 1.2m (4ft) square of wall, brush on the diluted paint from every direction in large sweeping movements.

4 Softening the brush strokes Using a dry brush, work over the wet section of wall to blur or remove any hard and obvious brush marks. Dry the brush regularly by wiping it on a rag.

THE PROFESSIONAL FINISH

For a more translucent, tougher finish than emulsion (latex), try colourwashing with a special solvent/oil-based scumble glaze which is available from art supply shops. You can use the glaze on all interior walls and woodwork, but as it's more expensive than emulsion and is very durable, it's particularly suitable for colourwashing a small area that comes in for heavy wear, such as a door. Because of its base, a scumble glaze would also suit a condensation-prone zone such as a bathroom or kitchen. To use the glaze, dilute with white (mineral) spirit and colour it by adding solvent/oil-based eggshell. For a base coat use solvent/oil-based eggshell, or vinyl silk emulsion (satin latex) for areas of less heavy wear.

A pale wash of cool sea-blue over white gives translucent depth to this wall. All you need for this sort of colourwashing is emulsion (latex) paint and water, and the technique couldn't be simpler. The wash is vigorously swept over the surface and then brushed out to reveal some of the base colour.

5 **Checking the effect** When you have completed a section, stand back and make sure that the paint is evenly dispersed. If you want to reveal more base colour, go over the wet paint again, using firm strokes with the dry brush to remove more paint. Continue across the wall, applying the wash and softening the brush strokes as you work, and making sure that you soften and blend in adjoining sections. Finish by brushing out excess paint at the edges of the wall, in corners or around doors and windows.

6 **Adding more colour (optional)** To add more depth and shade to the wall, wait until the first wash has dried then apply a second wash in a different colour. Simply repeat steps 2, 3, 4 and 5.

TIP

SOFTENING THE EFFECT
For a softer overall effect, use a dry piece of cotton rag to wipe away the colourwash and blur the brush strokes. Follow steps 1-3, then fold a clean rag into a loose pad to wipe the wet wall, using a mixture of dabbing and light rubbing movements. Because the amount of base coat revealed can be more carefully controlled than with a brush, the rag method is especially useful for a small area such as a door.

PAINTING A BLANKET BOX

If you want to experiment with colourwashing but would rather begin with a small project, try your hand at painting a piece of wooden furniture like a blanket box or small cupboard.

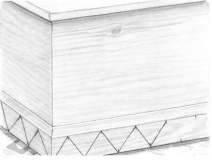

A wash of soft green emulsion over a base coat of pale blue, combined with a cheerful zigzag border, gives a new lease of life to a blanket box. A name picked out in border colours on the lid is a nice personal touch.

1 Preparing the box Protect the working area with plenty of plastic sheets or newspaper, then sand smooth any painted or varnished surfaces on the box and fill any cracks with wood filler. Sand smooth again and wipe off dust with a cloth. If necessary, apply white wood primer to seal any bare wood.

2 Marking off the border Measure and mark a pencil line all round the box about 10cm (4in) from the base. Mark alternate equal distances along the line and the base of the box and join up the points in a zigzag pattern. Cover the top of the border with masking tape.

3 Applying the paint Brush a base coat of pale blue over the whole box, stopping at the masking tape. Leave to dry. Dilute one part green paint with four parts water and brush the wash quickly all over the base coat down to the masking tape.

4 Softening the lines Using a dry brush or cotton rag, work over the painted surfaces to soften the brush strokes and reveal some of the base coat.

5 Wiping the edges Wrap a clean cloth tightly around your forefinger then, using your nail to create a sharp edge, wipe the wash off the edge of the lid and the strip above the border. Wipe smoothly and cleanly, trying not to smudge the colourwash, then leave to dry.

6 Painting in the pattern Remove the masking tape from the base and use the smaller brush to paint in the triangles with different coloured paint. Don't worry if the lines between the colours are not completely straight and crisp – soft lines only add to the charm.

BLOCK PRINTING

The simplest of printing methods, block printing
makes ingenious use of everyday materials to add pattern and colour
to walls and accessories around your home.

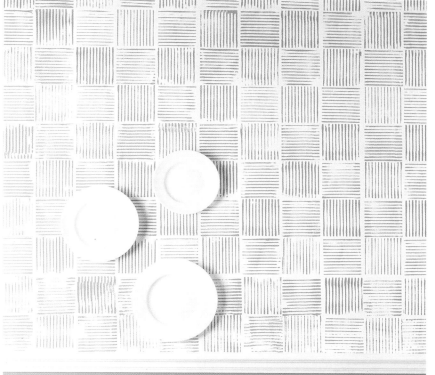

W ith its pleasant, handcrafted look, block printing is a fun way of creating patterns or adding a texture to items around your home. The block simply describes the item that you print with – traditionally it would have been a motif carved out of a wooden block, but it is possible to improvise. A shape can be carved out of the surface of soft materials such as sponge or potatoes, or a textured material mounted on to a wooden block. Then you simply apply paint to the block and stamp your design directly on to the surface to be decorated.

Part of the fun of block printing lies in experimenting with different materials. Many objects commonly found around the house can be used – try the end of a cork from a bottle, a sponge, an offcut of carpet, old table mat, corrugated cardboard or even scraps of textured wallpaper. Some materials, such as wallpaper, need to be mounted on to a small block of wood or sanding block so that they are easy to hold while printing; others, like a sponge, work well without a block.

Pleasing and dramatic effects can be created by using just one colour. And, as handprinting is always irregular, don't worry if each print is slightly different, as any variations will add to the final effect. Walls, furniture, accessories or fabric can be decorated this way, whether you print the entire item with repeated motifs, print just one motif or create a border. Before you start, experiment first on scrap paper.

You can achieve a stylish result at little cost and with the simplest of materials – here, prints from corrugated cardboard taped to a wooden block create a pleasing chequerboard effect.

PRINTING TECHNIQUES

The basic techniques of block printing are the same whatever you choose to print and use as a block. The steps below show printing with a sponge – if you use a material that needs to be mounted on a block, prepare the block first then proceed with the steps. Always mark out and prepare the area to be painted with care, and make a few practice prints on scrap paper. Protect your finished design with a coat of varnish.

SUITABLE PAINTS

Many paints can be used for block printing – but for the best results the paint should be the consistency of thick cream. Special block printing paints are available from artists' supply shops. These have the right creamy consistency and do not dry too quickly on the block, so they give a well defined print. Artist's acrylics and children's PVA paints are suitable and it is also

possible to use water-based household paints such as matt emulsion (flat latex). Tester pots of emulsion are an ideal size for first time or small scale projects.

MAKING A BLOCK

Blocks can be made by carving into the surface of wood, lino or materials such as sponge or potato. Alternatively, mount soft items such as string or carpet, or those which cannot be easily held, on to a separate piece of wood using a waterproof glue. Pliable materials, such as textured wallpaper or card, can be wrapped around a block and taped in place.

APPLYING THE PAINT

One of the best ways of applying the paint to the block is with a small roller, from an art shop, which coats the paint evenly over the surface. A brush can be used, but not as

▶ *A simple chequerboard sponge print sealed with several coats of varnish makes a handsome splashback to this sink – follow the steps below to experiment with the technique.*

effectively. Or you can dip the block into a dish of paint – this is the easiest way to coat soft surfaces such as sponge, but dab off excess paint on scrap paper before printing.

PREPARING THE SURFACE

The surface must be sound, clean and free of grease. Wash down walls or furniture with a mild solution of (sugar) soap or detergent, and allow them to dry thoroughly before printing. If the paint is flaking or peeling it should be removed and the surface repainted.

SPONGE PRINTING

A household synthetic sponge can be used as a square as shown here, or carved into shapes with a craft knife. The steps show a chequerboard effect being practised on a sheet of card.

YOU WILL NEED

- ❖ RULE, PENCIL
- ❖ MASKING TAPE
- ❖ SYNTHETIC SPONGE cut into a 15cm (6in) square
- ❖ EMULSION (LATEX) PAINT, in blue or colour of your choice
- ❖ OLD PLATE large enough to take the sponge
- ❖ SCRAP PAPER
- ❖ CLEAR, water-based VARNISH and BRUSH

1 Positioning the design Use a rule and pencil to work out where you want the first row of squares to start. Mark this position with masking tape.

2 Positioning the motifs Using the sponge as a template, mark off the position of the chequer pattern along the edge of the masking tape.

3 Applying the paint Pour a small amount of paint on to the plate. Lightly press the sponge into the paint and dab off any excess on to scrap paper.

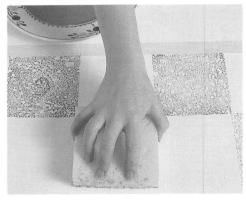

4 Making prints Working from just above the tape upwards, press the sponge on the card, matching the corners to the guide marks. Re-apply the paint if necessary, then print again, a blank square away from the first one. Print the first row then continue the chequer pattern by alternating the order of printed squares in each row.

5 Finishing When the design has dried, apply two or three coats of clear, water-based varnish, allowing it to dry completely between coats.

PRINT EFFECTS

As a first time project, try your hand on something small such as a tray, blanket box, border or frieze. Simple geometric patterns often work best — as your skills develop you may want to progress to a more complex, freer style of design.

▶ *Dramatic in its simplicity, this handpainted yellow border has been sponge printed with rectangles in a contrasting colour.*

◀ *A section of sisal matting was used as a central motif on this tray, and the finished design sealed with varnish. For fun coordination, print the design on accessories such as paper napkins.*

▼ *Experiment with improvised printing materials, from textured wallpaper and cardboard to table mats. A roller helps load paint evenly on to your printing block.*

PAINTING STRIPES

Painted stripes add impact to walls and make a lively change from plain backgrounds. They're easy to paint if you use masking tape to guide you along the edges.

D epending on the colours, proportions and paint finish, painted stripes on walls can give a number of different effects – from subtle, classic and elegant to bold, jazzy and modern. You can use bright, clashing colours or mellow, toning combinations, either applied as flat colour or with a paint effect, such as sponging, dragging or stippling, for a softer finish.

Really dramatic striped effects are best reserved for less frequently used rooms, such as dining rooms, where you can enjoy them without having to live with them all day, or for children's rooms where they'll create a fun, stimulating backdrop. Subtler looks, such as honey beige stripes over a cream base, fit in anywhere.

For the look to succeed, the stripes need to be absolutely vertical or horizontal, and perfectly parallel. You can achieve this with careful measuring and marking up, using a plumb line for vertical stripes and a level for horizontal ones. For the neatest outline, use masking tape to define the edges of the stripes. If you live in an old house, take a good look at the walls before you begin – if they're very irregular and slope at the corners, you might need to reconsider using stripes as they emphasize any imperfections.

If you find all-over striped walls a trifle overpowering, opt for a stripy dado instead. In this sunny bedroom, wide lilac stripes painted over a green-grey base coat and topped with a horizontal band of peach give the dado the feeling of a balustrade.

PAINTING STRIPES ON TO A WALL

YOU WILL NEED

- ❖ FILLER
- ❖ EMULSION (LATEX) PAINT – one colour for the base coat and one or two other shade(s) for the stripes
- ❖ ROLLER to apply base coat
- ❖ PLUMB LINE
- ❖ MEASURING TAPE
- ❖ CHALK
- ❖ MASKING TAPE
- ❖ SPONGE
- ❖ SMALL PAINT BRUSH
- ❖ CRAFT KNIFE

When measuring and marking up the stripes, try to arrange them symmetrically around features such as fireplaces and windows to achieve a balanced effect. The easiest way to do this is to centre the first stripe then work out from it.

These steps are for vertical stripes sponged in two colours over the base coat, but are easily adapted for horizontal stripes. To mark up horizontal stripes, measure and mark down from the ceiling at several points to the height of the first key stripe. Join the marks using a level and straightedge. Measure up and down from this line for the other stripes.

▶ For details on sponging, see pages 7-10.

PLANNING A DESIGN

It's a good idea to plan your striped design before you begin. To make masking off easier, make the base colour stripes the same width as your masking tape – usually 2.5cm (1in), though you can buy wider widths. Also, if you leave a space between every painted stripe, as shown here, you only need to mask off the spaces – not the stripes themselves.

Draw a section of the design to scale on a large piece of paper and colour it in. Hold it up to the wall to check the effect. If it's a bold design, leave it there for a few days to make sure you don't tire of it.

1 Applying the base coat Prepare the walls, filling any cracks and holes. Use the roller to apply the base coat, then leave it to dry thoroughly.

2 Marking up the stripes Measure the width of the wall (or of the feature on which you want to centre the stripes) and mark the mid-point. Hang a plumb line from the ceiling at this point. Use the chalk to mark small dots on to the wall at intervals down the plumb line. This line indicates the *centre* of your first stripe. Following your design, measure and mark out from the dots on each side to mark up the stripe widths across the wall, using a plumb line at intervals to check the stripes are vertical.

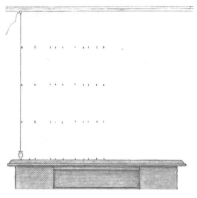

3 Dealing with corners As you work towards the corners, plan ahead to make sure you have a full stripe on each side; this often involves making slight adjustments to the width of the stripes running up to the corner, but this won't be noticeable in the end result.

4 Masking off Use masking tape to mask off the stripes you want to remain the base colour, lining up the tape edges with the chalk dots. Keep the tape taut to prevent wrinkles and press it down firmly. On wide stripes, there's no need to mask off the whole stripe – just the side edges.

5 Applying the paint Following your design, carefully sponge your first paint colour on to all the unmasked stripes to be painted in this shade, taking the paint just over the tape edges. Clean the sponge thoroughly then use it to apply the second colour to the remaining unmasked stripes.

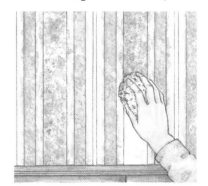

Use stripes of different widths and colours to build up attractive designs, like this elegant combination of mint green and lavender stripes. The stripes are sponged over a lavender-blue tinted white background in this sequence: 4cm (1½in) wide mint stripe, 2.5cm (1in) space, 8cm (3in) wide lavender stripe, 2.5cm (1in) space, 4cm (1½in) wide mint stripe, 6cm (2¼in) space.

6 Removing the tape When the paint is touch-dry, gently but steadily pull away the tape. If any of the base coat starts peeling away with it, stop and use a craft knife to slit along the edge of the lifting paint to release it and stop it lifting all along the stripe. Continue removing the tape. Touch up any areas where the paint has lifted with a small paint brush. Leave the wall to dry thoroughly. Brush off any chalk marks.

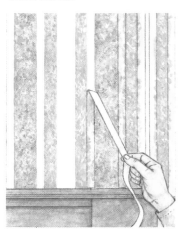

Painting stripes on to your wall, rather than using a wallpaper, gives you the freedom to create any design you like – and at a fraction of the cost of paper. Here are some ideas to inspire you.

▶ *A lounge with a seashore theme is set off perfectly by watery blue waves rippling across white walls. To copy this look, chalk a guideline on to the wall to indicate the centre of each wave; then paint a wavy line along each guideline, using a brush the desired width of the wave. Stop the waves at dado height so the effect isn't too overpowering.*

▼ *Wide stripes in bold primaries over a white background create a playful, circus-like atmosphere in a child's bedroom. For a textured finish, the stripes are applied using a lightly coated paint roller.*

▲ *Add a striking, contemporary look to your bathroom with evenly spaced stripes painted in vivid blue or another bright colour over a fresh white background. Choose accessories to match for a coordinated finish, and soften the effect with vases of fresh flowers.*

OIL GLAZE WORK

Oil glaze work, also known as scumble glazing, creates a softened broken-colour finish on walls and furniture. The effect enriches the surfaces, giving them depth, movement and texture.

W orking with oil glazes may sound technical, but the process is really quite straightforward and the richness of the results definitely speaks for itself. Oil or scumble glaze is simply a transparent medium which you tint to the required shade with artists' oil colours. When applied over an oil-based basecoat, such as eggshell paint, the glaze spreads a soft, cloudy veil of colour over the underlying paint, creating a depth, movement and character not achievable with broken-colour effects worked with opaque paints.

By varying the application of the techniques and the colours and the surfaces on which you are working very different styles are created. These can range from a distressed, rustic style to a richer, sophisticated town house look. You can apply the techniques to both old and new walls and woodwork – the effects look different but equally good. Imperfections on older and roughened surfaces give a more textured, country farmhouse look, whereas when the technique is applied to smooth surfaces, a richer, smarter look is introduced into a room setting.

A vibrant viridian green glaze brushed over a buttermilk basecoat on the walls of this bathroom creates an evocative backdrop, reminiscent of the gently rippling surface of the sea.

OIL-GLAZING TECHNIQUES

The technique involves applying the glaze over the basecoat with a brush, then working over the wet glaze with either a brush or a cloth. Very different effects are achieved depending on how you work the glaze and what you use to work it. As a general guideline, a cloth creates a rough, natural texture, while a brush can give a very controlled, neat finish.

A popular way of finishing the glaze with a brush is to use a stippling technique. This gives a subtle, fine texture that is particularly suited to smaller areas or items, such as the skirting and architrave in a room or on furniture. The process involves using a dry, decorators' softening brush in a dabbing motion over the wet glaze. More information about stippling is given overleaf.

MIXING COLOURS

The best effects are created by applying the tinted glaze over a white or pale base coat. To tint a glaze, you can mix any number of artists' oil colours in varying amounts to achieve your desired shade. To create a feeling of depth you can apply two tinted glazes in different colours over the base coat. You can closely link the colours of the glazes, using, for example, a light shade followed by a darker, harmonious shade, or for a more dramatic effect you can use contrasting colour glazes, such as a blue over yellow. It is always advisable to experiment on a spare piece of board before starting a project, to make sure you like the effect your chosen colour combination produces.

When painting walls, it's important to mix sufficient coloured glaze to cover the desired area, as you will find it difficult to re-mix and obtain the same colour later. As a guide, two litres of mixed, coloured glaze covers a room measuring 4.5m (15ft) square with ease. It is a good idea to work on one wall at a time, as this allows enough time for you to perfect the finish before the glaze dries.

YOU WILL NEED

- ❖ WHITE, FLAT OIL-BASED UNDERCOAT PAINT
- ❖ PAINT BRUSH OR PAINT TRAY AND ROLLER
- ❖ PAINT KETTLE
- ❖ OIL (SCUMBLE) GLAZE
- ❖ WHITE (MINERAL) SPIRIT
- ❖ ARTISTS' OIL PAINTS
- ❖ OLD JAR for measuring
- ❖ PALETTE KNIFE OR SMALL KNIFE for mixing paint
- ❖ CONTAINERS for mixed glazes
- ❖ LARGE DECORATORS' PAINT BRUSH
- ❖ HOG HAIR OR BADGER SOFTENING BRUSH
- ❖ SOFT MUSLIN CLOTH (optional)
- ❖ OIL-BASED MATT OR SATIN VARNISH

This effect is created with two toning green glazes over a white basecoat. Mix the tints for the glazes using artists' oil colours as follows: for the bright green glaze, mix 3 parts emerald green, 3 parts bright green and 1 part raw umber with a little white (mineral) spirit; for the dark green glaze, mix 3 parts terre vert, 2 parts viridian, 1 part raw umber, 1 part Paynes grey with a little white (mineral) spirit. Add to the prepared oil glaze in the ratio 1 part colour to 8 parts oil glaze medium.

1 Applying the base coat Prepare the wall surface, making good any loose plaster, filling cracks and removing any flaky paint. Using a brush or a paint tray and short-pile roller, paint the walls with two coats of white, oil-based undercoat. Allow to dry.

2 Mixing the oil glaze medium Mix equal parts of oil-based glaze and white (mineral) spirit in the paint kettle. Stir thoroughly.

3 Mixing the first glaze In a paint kettle or tray, mix together artists' oil paints and a little white (mineral) spirit to the desired shade. Use a knife to mix this to a smooth, thick consistency.

4 Adding the oil glaze medium Using a clean paint tray or other suitable container, measure and pour in one part ready-mixed colour followed by eight parts oil glaze medium and mix well. At this stage the consistency should be like thin cream.

5 Applying the first glaze With a large, standard decorators' paint brush, roughly brush the tinted glaze over the wall in broad random strokes, crossing over your previous brush marks and leaving small spaces to show the white base coat.

6 Softening the brush marks Quickly pass a clean, dry softening brush (or cloth) over the glaze, blurring the brush marks and softly pushing the glaze over the small, unglazed spaces. Aim to create areas of darker and lighter tones. Allow to dry for 24 hours.

7 Mixing the second glaze Following steps 3 and 4, use darker shades of artists' oil paint to create a second tinted glaze.

8 **Applying the second glaze** Apply the second glaze as in step 5, but in this case leave slightly larger spaces between the brush strokes, to expose softened areas of the lighter glaze. Soften the effect as in step 6, to create a subtle, mottled effect in varying tones.

9 **Protecting the finish** To protect and enhance the oil glaze work, when the coloured glaze is thoroughly dry, apply two coats of clear varnish, allowing each one to dry between applications. A matt varnish gives a natural look, whereas a satin finish gives a sheen.

TIP

GLAZE RATIOS

For the best effects, mix the coloured glazes in the following ratios:

Walls: when mixing a glaze for walls, mix the tinted glaze in a ratio of 1 part ready-mixed colour to 8 parts prepared oil glaze medium.

Wood: when mixing glaze to stipple on woodwork and furniture, mix the tinted glaze in a ratio of 1 part ready-mixed colour to 3 parts prepared oil glaze medium.

STIPPLE-GLAZED TRAY

A stippled effect is a hardwearing finish to use on wooden kitchen accessories. To paint a wooden tray in the same way as the one shown here, as well as the materials listed on the previous page, you need a 2.5-5cm (1-2in) household paint brush. To copy the colour effect, mix the first glaze using 6 parts white, 2 parts Prussian blue, 2 parts raw umber and 1 part yellow ochre artists' oil paint and adding oil glaze medium. Make the second glaze by adding oil glaze medium to permanent blue artists' oil paint.

Choose colours from soft furnishings to decorate your accessories – this tray is stipple-glazed to match the table cloth.

1 **Preparing the wooden tray** Prepare the surface, then paint both sides with white oil-based undercoat, allowing the paint on one side to dry before painting the other. When dry, work the different stages of the glazed effect given below in the same way, on one side of the tray at a time.

2 **Applying the first glaze** Mix up the glazes as in *Oil-glazing Techniques*, steps 2-4, but in a ratio of 1 part colour to 3 parts oil glaze. Using a household paint brush, apply the first glaze sparingly, following the direction of the wood grain.

3 **Stippling the glaze** While the glaze is still wet, take a dry, clean, hog hair softening brush and dab this quickly in and out of the glaze. Continue until all the brush marks have disappeared and there are tiny soft dotted marks over the whole surface. Allow to dry thoroughly.

4 **Applying the second glaze** Apply the second glaze as the first. Using a dry, clean hog hair softening brush, stipple away brush marks so the glaze blends with the underlying colour. Stipple more heavily in some areas to create a shaded effect. Allow to dry.

5 **Protecting the surface** Paint two coats of matt or satin varnish over the glazed tray, allowing each one to dry thoroughly.

RAGGING

Ragging is a broken colour technique which creates a random pattern that echoes crushed velvet. This quick and easy paint effect is ideal for walls or fitted furniture such as a run of cupboards.

I t's easy to get a pleasing result with ragging – a quick paint technique which uses rags to make patterns in thinned paint. The random pattern is perfect for adding interest to a large expanse of wall and is useful for disguising uneven or blemished surfaces. You can also use it when you want an interesting finish on smaller areas such as kitchen units, skirting boards and shelves.

Ragging requires very little equipment. All you need is two colours of a paint suitable for the surface, a roller, a paint brush and plenty of clean rags. Emulsion (latex) is usually the best choice of paint for a large area such as a wall. The technique can be used to produce a wide range of effects depending on the colours you choose, the sort of rag you use and how tightly you gather it up.

Ragging can be subtle or intense depending on your choice of colours. Here a sunny yellow ragged over white produces a cheerful result in a kitchen.

RAGGING TECHNIQUES

There are three methods of ragging: ragging off, ragging on and rag rolling. Whichever method you choose, one or two coats of a base colour must be applied first and allowed to dry. When ragging, the pattern is affected by the way the rag is scrunched. The tighter the rag, the more dense the pattern will be. It's important to keep to the same degree of scrunching over a whole wall to avoid a patchy effect.

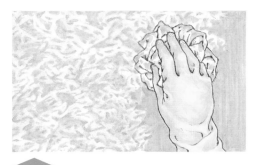

Ragging off is the most commonly used method. After allowing the base coat to dry, paint on a coat of thinned emulsion (latex) in a second colour. Scrunch up a rag and press it on to the wet painted surface to make a random pattern by removing some of the thinned paint to reveal patches of the base colour.

Ragging on produces a more pronounced pattern than ragging off. Once the base coat is dry simply scrunch up a dry rag and use it to apply the thinned emulsion (latex) in a second colour.

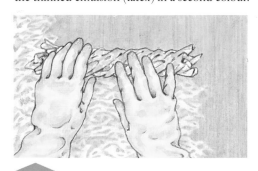

Rag rolling produces a more regular pattern than other methods. It should be done in vertical lines to produce an even effect. The thinned emulsion is first applied over the dried base coat as for ragging off. Then the rag is bunched into a sausage shape and lightly rolled up the wall in one movement to form a mottled strip. This rolling is repeated over the wall.

CHOOSING COLOURS

When planning your colour scheme, bear in mind that the best results are usually created by using a light shade for the base colour and ragging or rag rolling a darker shade over the top. Before you begin to paint a wall, buy some tester pots of paint and experiment with different colours on a sheet of lining paper. Stick the lining paper up on the wall with masking tape to check the result in natural and artificial light.

The safest way to achieve a successful result is to combine two tones of one colour; try peach ragged over pale apricot for a warm look or use a strong blue over a paler blue for a cooler effect. Avoid colours which are very close in tone or next to each other on the shade card, as these may be too similar for the effect to show up.

By experimenting with colour combinations you can create different effects. Pale grey or blue looks good over white for a pastel colour scheme; apricot over cream will have more of a cosy feel. Lime green over lemon yellow will produce a vibrant scheme. To create really dramatic effects choose strong colours such as wine or a fresh green over white or ivory.

CHOOSING RAGS

Unglazed cotton is the traditional material for ragging, and old cotton sheets are perfect. For a softer effect you could also try cheesecloth, or a roll of decorator's cloth. Synthetic fabrics such as polyester are not suitable because they don't absorb the paint. Fabrics with a small amount of synthetic fibres such as a cotton/polyester blend would still work, but with less definition than pure cotton.

Experiment with different fabrics scrunched up tightly or held more loosely until you get the effect you want. Make sure you have a plentiful supply of cloths as the rags soon become clogged with paint – an ideal size is about 20 x 30cm (8 x 12in). Cut the cloth up into useable sizes before you start ragging – you must work quickly, particularly with the ragging off technique.

▶ *Deep peach emulsion was ragged over a very pale peach base coat, leaving a pattern and revealing areas of pale colour underneath.*

RAGGING A WALL

Before painting, first carefully prepare the walls by filling any cracks and holes and sanding rough areas where necessary. The instructions opposite are for ragging off, but you can experiment with the variations of ragging on or rag rolling – see the instructions under Ragging Techniques above.

With ragging, the paint needs to be worked before it dries. If you are working by yourself, it is best to apply the thinned paint to one section of the wall at a time, then rag over it before moving on to the next section. If you can get a friend to help, one person can work ahead, applying the thinned paint, and the other can follow behind with the rag, removing some of the wet paint.

YOU WILL NEED

- ❖ RUBBER GLOVES
- ❖ EMULSION (LATEX) PAINT
- ❖ PAINT ROLLER and TRAY
- ❖ PAINT KETTLE
- ❖ 8cm (3in) PAINT BRUSH
- ❖ CLEAN RAGS

1 Applying the base coat Using a roller, apply a coat of the base colour. When this is dry, if necessary paint on a second coat. Allow to dry thoroughly before starting the ragging process.

3 Ragging off Scrunch up a rag and dab it lightly and quickly on to the wall, removing some of the thinned paint. Vary the direction of your hand and adjust the rag occasionally for a random pattern.

2 Applying the top coat In a paint kettle, gradually add water to emulsion (latex) paint in your second colour until the paint is thinner than the consistency of single cream. Brush the thinned paint over the base coat, working quickly over one section of the wall at a time.

4 Checking the effect Continue working over the wall, one section at a time. Stand back from the wall at intervals to check the result, and lightly touch in any missed areas. When the rag becomes clogged with paint, use a fresh rag or rinse it with water and squeeze out the excess before continuing.

RAGGING CUPBOARD DOORS

▲ These kitchen units have been given a fresh coat of grey-green paint. The decorative detail is brought out by ragging inside the panels and using a brush stroke technique elsewhere.

Before you start on a large expanse of wall, you may prefer to experiment with a smaller ragging project such as wooden cupboard doors or kitchen units – the technique is just as successful over wood as over walls. The method is the same except that a tougher water-based or solvent-based satin finish paint is used instead of emulsion.

Ragging looks effective when used together with another paint technique. The cupboard door and drawer panels illustrated here have been ragged while the rest of the unit has been given a different finish, achieved by slowly and firmly dragging a paint brush over the surface in one direction so that the brush strokes are clearly visible.

All cupboards and units should be well cleaned before painting. Remove handles, then wash down doors and frames with hot soapy water. When dry, wipe over with methylated spirit (denatured alcohol).

YOU WILL NEED

- ❖ RUBBER GLOVES
- ❖ 5cm (2in) PAINT BRUSH
- ❖ WOOD PRIMER
- ❖ SATIN FINISH PAINT
- ❖ MASKING TAPE
- ❖ PAINT KETTLE
- ❖ WHITE (MINERAL) SPIRIT or WATER
- ❖ RAGS

1 Painting the base
Apply a coat of primer on new or bare wood. When dry, paint on a coat of satin finish paint in the base colour. Allow to dry. Mask off the area around the panels.

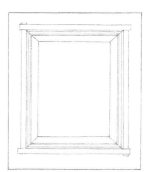

2 Applying the paint
Thin paint in the second colour with water or white (mineral) spirit (depending on if it's water- or solvent/oil-based), just thinner than single cream. Use paint brush to apply even coat to one panel.

3 Ragging the surface Scrunch up a clean dry cloth to the required tightness and dab it on to the thinned wet paint to leave a ragged pattern.

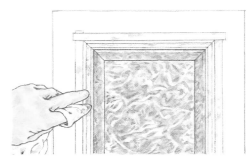

4 Picking out the moulding
Wrap your index finger in a clean piece of cloth and run it carefully around the moulded part of the door, to remove any thinned paint. Apply paint and rag off other panels in the same way. Leave to dry.

5 Painting panel surround
(optional) Remove all masking tape. Apply a coat of thinned paint to areas around the panel and then draw a clean, dry brush slowly and firmly over the surface in one direction, leaving brush marks. Let paint dry.

DRAGGING

Dragging is a subtle paint technique that can give a new lease of life to an inexpensive piece of old furniture and add a unique decorative finish to the walls and woodwork in your home.

Dragging is a traditional decorative paint finish similar to woodgraining. To achieve the attractive streaky effect you apply a semi-transparent glaze over a different base colour. Then you pull or drag a dry brush across the wet glaze so that some of it is removed to reveal thin lines of the base colour underneath.

In the eighteenth and nineteenth centuries, dragging was a popular way of making simple wooden furniture look more like the elaborate mahogany wardrobes and sideboards in grander homes. Interior designers no longer try to make dragging look like fake wood grain. Instead, it is used to add rich layers of colour and interesting surface texture to walls, doors and window frames, as well as furniture.

Different colour combinations create different moods – a pastel glaze over a white ground looks fresh in a bedroom or bathroom, whereas light and dark shades of a warm colour such as terracotta give a living room a welcoming glow.

The following pages show how to drag a wall, and how to drag a plain wooden box in an attractive striped design.

Walls dragged with a bright blue glaze over a pale blue base coat create an elegant backdrop for blue and white furnishings in this living room.

DRAGGING A WALL

You'll find it much easier to drag a wall if you have a helper. One of you can apply the glaze in bands about 60cm (2ft) wide, and the other can follow on behind to drag it. Keep the glaze well brushed out so that it doesn't run, and try to drag from the top to the bottom of the wall in one motion, so that the vertical stripes are continuous. If you cannot drag down the wall in one go, stop and restart the dragging fairly low down where the 'join' won't be so noticeable. Do not stop and start at the same place each time.

The steps below explain the technique for dragging using an eggshell base coat and an oil-based glaze. If you want to use water-based paints, mix and tint the glaze according to the manufacturer's instructions and follow the same steps.

PAINTS

You can either use oil- or solvent-based paints or water-based paints for dragging. The only thing you must not do is mix the two different types of paint, as they are incompatible. Most professional decorators use solvent-based paints because they are slow-drying and produce a more clearly defined dragged effect than water-based paints.

Choose eggshell paint for the background colour and an oil-based glaze (sometimes called a *scumble glaze*) for the top coat. Oil-based glaze is available from specialist decorating shops. It is fairly thick and creamy yellow in colour but dries to a transparent finish. Thin it down with an equal amount of white (mineral) spirit, and colour it with eggshell paint or artist's oil paints.

If you prefer to use water-based paints, use emulsion (latex) paint for the background colour and an acrylic scumble glaze for the top coat. Thin the glaze according to the manufacturer's instructions and tint it to the colour you want with either gouache paint, acrylic paint or a water-based tinting colour.

Whichever type of paint you choose, experiment with the colours on scrap paper until you are happy with the effect.

BRUSHES

The base coat and the glaze are both applied with ordinary decorating brushes – choose a size that suits the area you are working on. Use synthetic bristles for applying water-based paints.

Traditionally, the dragging is done with a dragging brush (sometimes called a 'flogger'). Dragging brushes have long, evenly spaced bristles and come in various sizes from 7.5cm (3in) to 15cm (6in) wide. They are expensive, but it's worth investing in a large one if you want to decorate a couple of rooms. A cheaper brush that is normally used for hanging wallpaper is also reasonably effective over a smaller area.

YOU WILL NEED

- ❖ PLASTIC SHEETING OR NEWSPAPER
- ❖ EGGSHELL PAINT
- ❖ OIL-BASED GLAZE
- ❖ WHITE (MINERAL) SPIRIT
- ❖ ARTISTS' OIL PAINT
- ❖ BUCKET (for mixing up glaze)
- ❖ DECORATING BRUSH
- ❖ DRAGGING BRUSH
- ❖ RAG to wipe brush
- ❖ POLYURETHANE VARNISH

1 Preparing the wall Make sure that the wall surface is smooth and even, and that it is clean and free from loose particles; rub over the wall with a clean duster if necessary.

2 Painting the base coat Apply the eggshell base coat with a decorating brush, and leave until completely dry.

3 Mixing the glaze Mix equal parts of glaze and white (mineral) spirit. Colour the glaze with artists' oil paint thinned with a little white (mineral) spirit. Pour paint into glaze gradually, and mix it in very well.

4 Applying the glaze Starting at one end of the wall, use a decorating brush to apply a smooth band of glaze, about 60cm (2ft) wide, over the base coat.

5 **Dragging the glaze** Work while the glaze is still wet. Hold the dragging brush so that the bristle tips just touch the glaze. Starting at the top of the wall, draw the brush firmly down the glaze with even pressure so that stripes of the base colour show through. Wipe the dragging brush with a rag now and then so that it stays dry. Repeat steps 4 and 5 until you have dragged the whole wall.

6 **Varnishing** Allow the glaze to dry completely. If you wish, you can finish the wall with one or two coats of varnish – this isn't essential, but gives the wall a more durable finish.

A yellowy-green glaze dragged over a white background gives this wall a fresh and tangy finish with an attractive texture. Avoid dragging rough, uneven walls, as the fine lines produced tend to highlight surface irregularities.

DRAGGING A WOODEN BOX

1 Preparing the box If your box has a hinged lid, remove it with a small screwdriver. Paint the box and lid with one coat of primer. When dry, paint with one coat of white satin finish paint. Leave to dry.

2 Painting the moulding Paint any moulding on the box and lid in your two chosen colours (purple and green are used here). Leave the box to dry.

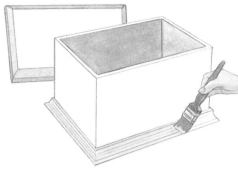

☑ *Dragging on wood is usually worked following the grain; here, however, it's worked across it to create an interesting criss-crossing of textures.*

3 Masking off the stripes Decide on the width of the stripes to go on the sides and lid of the box. Use a pencil and ruler to lightly mark them out. Cover alternate stripes with masking tape.

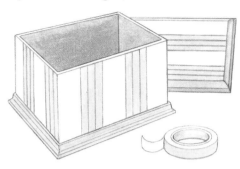

4 Painting the first colour stripes Mix up the glaze in your first chosen colour. Working on one side of the box at a time, apply the glaze with a decorating brush and soften out the brush strokes with an artists' fan tail brush. Leave the glaze for ten minutes so that it sets slightly. Drag each stripe with a dragging brush, starting at the bottom and dragging up to the top. Carefully remove the masking tape while the paint is still wet. Repeat on the box lid. Leave the box to dry for 24 hours.

5 Painting the second colour stripes Mix up the glaze in your second colour. Apply the glaze to the remaining stripes and drag them, as in step 4. If any of the second colour glaze runs over the first colour stripes, wrap a piece of soft rag around your finger and gently wipe it off. Leave the paint to dry. Screw on the lid. Varnish the box.

Preparing walls

Good preparation is essential to success when repainting.

It takes time to prepare wall and ceiling surfaces thoroughly, but a smooth, clean surface ensures that the new paint flows on easily and evenly and adheres properly. The first step is to examine the walls and ceiling to assess their condition and establish what preparation is needed.
See pages 73-74 for removing wallcoverings.

Assessing the surface

Clean paintwork If the surfaces have been painted before, and the paintwork is sound, all they need is a wash with detergent or (sugar) soap and a rinse with clean water, followed by a light sanding to prepare them for the new paint.

Damaged paintwork Scrape or sand off any cracking, flaking or peeling paint and touch in the low spots with some paint or filler to avoid leaving a depression that might show through the new paint.

Cracks in plaster A coat of paint usually fills hairline cracks, especially if you use a textured paint. But you should fill cracks wider than 1mm (1⁄16in) especially those along the wall or ceiling junction, or the joins between plasterboard sheets. Also fill any cracks along the edges of skirting boards or door architraves. Repair dents, holes or other damage to the surfaces that you find during your inspection.

Wallcoverings Remove wallcoverings

before painting, unless they are designed to be overpainted – a woodchip (ingrain) or relief paper, for example. Treat these as you would painted plaster, by washing and rinsing the surface. Stick down any lifting seams before you start painting.

Other surfaces If the walls and ceilings have a textured finish, tiles, wallboards or cladding, you can either keep them, simply repainting them, or remove them and paint the surface below.

Cleaning sound paintwork

YOU WILL NEED

- ❖ PLASTIC SHEETS AND DUSTSHEETS
- ❖ WATERPROOF ADHESIVE TAPE
- ❖ DETERGENT OR (SUGAR) SOAP
- ❖ LONG-HANDLED MOP for ceilings
- ❖ GLOVES
- ❖ SAFETY GOGGLES (for washing ceilings)
- ❖ CLOTHS AND BUCKETS
- ❖ WALLPAPER REPAIR ADHESIVE
- ❖ SMALL PASTE BRUSH, SEAM ROLLER
- ❖ STRIPPING KNIFE
- ❖ WET-AND-DRY ABRASIVE PAPER, medium grade
- ❖ SANDING BLOCK
- ❖ PAINT
- ❖ SMALL PAINT BRUSH

1 Preparing to start Remove everything attached to the walls and clear the room of as much furniture as possible. (Leave ceiling-mounted light fittings in place). Tape or pin plastic sheets to the top edges of the skirting boards and lay dustsheets on top to absorb splashes. For complete safety, turn off the electricity supply at the mains; if that's not practicable, tape plastic bags over sockets and switches.

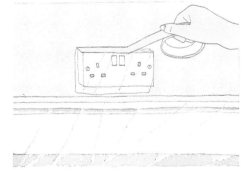

2 Washing the ceiling Using detergent or (sugar) soap in warm water and a long-handled mop, wash the ceiling. Move away from the main source of daylight to avoid working in your own shadow. Wear gloves and goggles so you don't get strong cleaning agents in your eyes. Rinse the surface, and leave to

3 Washing walls Start washing the walls at skirting board level and work upwards, then rinse with clean water working from the top down. Leave to dry.

4 Pasting down With a painted wallcovering, brush repair adhesive behind any seams or ends that have lifted. Allow the adhesive to soak into the back of the paper for a few minutes, then press the seam or edge back into place with a seam roller (but not on relief wallcoverings). If the paper has bubbled, slit the bubble, brush paste behind it and press down. Leave to dry for at least four hours before painting.

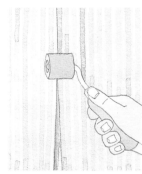

Repairing flaky paintwork

1 Removing old paint Use a stripping knife and medium-grade abrasive paper wrapped around a sanding block to remove any areas of flaky, blistered or peeling paint.

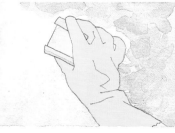

2 Filling Touch in the bare areas with a little paint to fill in the depression left behind. Apply a second or third coat if necessary. Use filler on deep holes – see overleaf.

Filling cracks and dents

Main surfaces

1 Preparing the surface Use the corner of a filling knife to open up very narrow cracks to give the filler something to hold on to. Blow or brush out any loose dust, and using an old paint brush, brush some water along the crack or into the hole to stop the filler drying out too quickly and cracking.

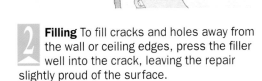

2 Filling To fill cracks and holes away from the wall or ceiling edges, press the filler well into the crack, leaving the repair slightly proud of the surface.

3 Sanding down When the filler has set hard, sand it down flush to the surrounding surface with abrasive paper wrapped around a sanding block.

Edge cracks

Use the materials described below rather than ordinary filler to repair cracks at the wall/ceiling join, at joins between sheets of plasterboard, or along the edges of skirting boards and door architraves. Ordinary filler will soon crack and fall out because of slight movement between the surfaces.

Filling joins

1 Using joint tape Rake out any loose material as above, then reinforce the angle between wall and ceiling, and any open joins between sheets of plasterboard, with self-adhesive joint tape.

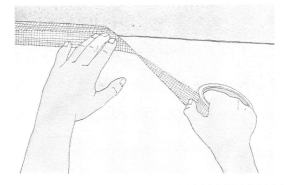

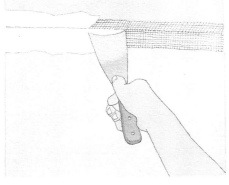

2 Concealing the tape Apply a skim of filler over the tape to conceal the open mesh. Paint over the filler when it has set, leaving a repair that won't crack again if movement re-occurs.

Filling gaps

1 Using a cartridge gun Place cartridge in gun with tip of nozzle cut. Squeeze trigger to force the mastic out. Press metal plate at back of gun to stop the mastic.

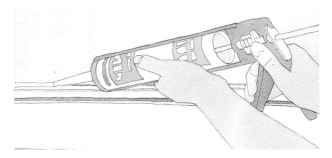

2 Using decorator's mastic Pipe the mastic between the wall and skirting boards or door architrave. Smooth it off neatly with a moistened finger. The mastic forms a surface skin which can be painted but which remains flexible, so preventing further cracks.

▼▼▼ TIP ▼▼▼

THE RIGHT CUT

Make the cartridge gun easier to use by cutting the tip of the nozzle off at an angle with a sharp craft knife – the further along the nozzle you make the cut, the larger the bead of mastic. For storage, push the cut off tip into the nozzle the other way round.

Painting: order of work

Working in a logical order saves time and effort, and gives a better result.

Woodwork around the home is subject to considerable wear and tear, and may well look as if it needs repainting before other surfaces require redecorating. Once your surface is well prepared, plan your order of work so that you are always working out from an edge that is still wet. For many wooden surfaces you may prefer to use varnish – the same rules apply.

If you're painting windows, or an external door, and don't want to leave them open overnight, start early in the morning and try to choose a fine, dry day. The room where you're painting must be well ventilated, so keep the windows and door open as much as possible.

Before you begin painting the walls or ceiling of a room, move all the furniture and ornaments out. If this is impractical, either position them in the middle of the room if there's enough space, or against one wall. You may have to paint one half of the room first, then move the furniture before you can do the other half, so think about the most logical place to put the furniture to save yourself moving it more than is absolutely necessary. If you do have to keep it inside the room you're painting, use plenty of dustsheets to protect it.

Order within a room

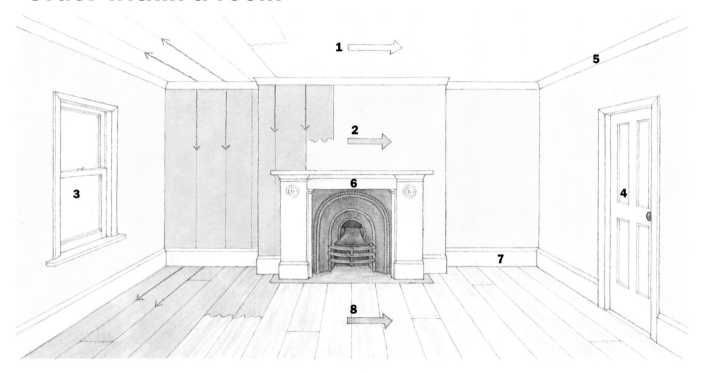

The illustration above charts the sequence of events when you are painting the entire room. Start by painting the ceiling, followed by the walls; in both cases work in overlapping bands, blending in the edges carefully. Paint away from the main source of natural light so that you can see clearly the area you've just painted.

Move on to the windows and doors (see overleaf). Next, paint any plasterwork details such as cornices or mouldings. Then tackle the fireplace, and finally the skirting boards and floor. Roll the carpet back from the skirting if possible. If not, use wide masking tape and a paint guard to protect the carpet as you work.

When you're not painting the whole room, simply follow the order given for the areas you do want to paint. Even when painting the individual elements in a room, follow the correct order of work to get the best finish.

Painting a staircase

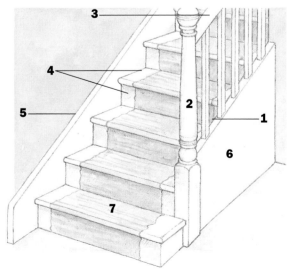

Work from the top down on each section, following the order shown. If you are laying a stair carpet, just paint the areas that will be exposed, but extend the paint to go at least 5cm (2in) under the carpet on each side.

Painting windows

Casement windows

Remove fittings if convenient. Protect the glass by stretching masking tape along the edge of the panes, but allow a gap of about 1.5mm (⅛in) between tape and wood so that the paint helps to seal the pane.

Have the opening casements wide open while you work, and follow the sequence in the diagram. Make sure that you paint any outside edges, too.

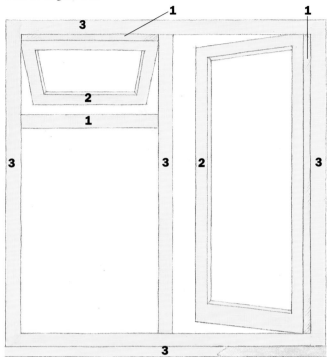

Sash windows

Protect the glass as described above. Then slide the top and bottom sashes up and down to expose different areas. Follow the sequence in the diagrams, taking care not to paint the sash cords.

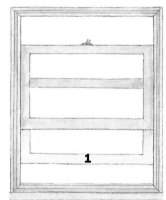

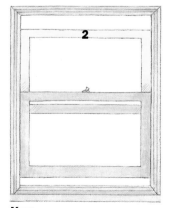
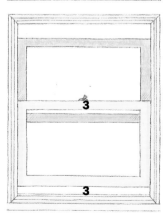
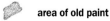

Key

 area to paint next

area of old paint

area already painted

Painting doors

Panelled doors

Start by removing all the door furniture and wedging the door open. Following the sequence shown in the diagram, work quickly to avoid join marks between sections. Finish each section with brush strokes along the grain of the wood – this means you have to use both vertical and horizontal strokes on a panelled door. At the end, remember to paint the rim of the door to match the room it opens into so that it blends with the decor.

Flush doors

Flush doors should be painted in one session, from top to bottom. Work quickly so that the edges stay wet. Keep your strokes long and light, and don't overbrush. Brush in from the edges, never towards them, or the paint will build up, run, and a ridge will form.

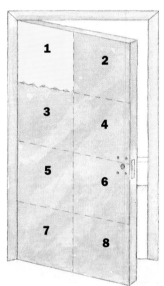

PAINTING IN TWO COLOURS

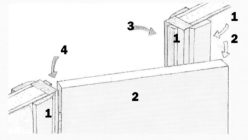

If you are painting your door different colours on either side, do the opening side first.
Paint the architrave and door frame up to and including the edge of the door stop (1) in your first colour. Then paint the face of the door and its opening edge (2) in the same colour.
Take your second colour and move to the opposite side of the door. Paint the architrave and frame up to and over the door stop (3). Finally, paint the opposite face of the door and its hinged edge (4) in the second colour.

Interior paints

Paint manufacturers have made great strides in recent years, and there is now a huge range to choose from.

Paint for indoors is mainly used as a decorative finish. But there are situations where special qualities are needed: paint on bathroom or kitchen walls, for example, has to stand up to condensation and be easy to clean.

When choosing paint it's important to bear in mind the type and finish.

Types of paint
Paints are divided into two basic categories: water-based and solvent/oil-based. The charts below and overleaf tell you where and how best to use them, but always check the label carefully for full instructions.

Water-based paints include vinyl emulsions (latex) for walls, and gloss and satin finishes for woodwork. Don't use emulsion (latex) over high gloss paint – it will not bond. Water-based paints are the simplest to work with: they are low-odour, easy to apply, fast-drying and tools can be cleaned in water.

Solvent/oil-based paints are the most hardwearing, durable group. However, they need more careful application and require cleaning up with white (mineral) spirit. They smell strongly and take time to dry. Primer is usually needed on bare surfaces. Undercoat is not necessary for one-coat paints.

Use solvent/oil-based paint with care: if painting in an enclosed space, keep the room well ventilated, do not leave the lid off the pot and don't smoke.

If you hate the smell or are allergic to solvent/oil-based paint, look for a water-based substitute.

Finishes
Water-based emulsion (latex) paints are available in matt (flat), silk (satin), semi-gloss and textured finishes for walls and ceilings; for wood, there are gloss and satin finishes with a water base. Painted emulsion surfaces range from spongeable to scrubbable.

Solvent/oil-based paints range from a subdued satin sheen to a hard, high gloss. High gloss is available in liquid and also non-drip forms.

Paints with a shine, including silk emulsion (satin latex), will highlight any surface defects but they are easier to keep clean than matt which turns shiny with frequent wiping.

Colour
Most paint finishes are available in a huge range of colours – either ready-mixed or custom-mixed from in-store tinting systems. Colour squares on shade cards are only an approximation of final colours, and they're so small that it is hard to imagine how they will look on an expanse of wall. Before making a decision, experiment with small test pots of colours in natural and artificial light.

Make sure you buy custom-mixed paint in one batch – getting a precise match from a second batch can never be guaranteed.

Before buying your tin of paint, check the charts below and overleaf to find out which paint to buy for the job.

The right paint for the surface

	Primer	Undercoat	Topcoat
Walls/Ceilings			
New plaster/plasterboard (leave to dry before using solvent/oil-based paint)	one sealing coat of thinned emulsion (latex) OR (alkali-resisting) primer	not needed	1 or 2 coats of emulsion (latex) OR solvent/oil-based paint
Sound, painted plaster	thinned coat of emulsion (latex) on bare areas OR (alkali-resisting) primer	not needed	1 or 2 coats of emulsion (latex) OR solvent/oil-based paint
Lining paper/Anaglypta	sealing coat of thinned emulsion (latex) if using solvent/oil–based paint	only under high gloss	1 or 2 coats of emulsion (latex) OR solvent/oil-based paint
Glazed tiles	zinc chromate primer	do not use undercoat	1 coat of solvent/oil-based full gloss paint
Wood			
Bare softwood/building boards	knotting over resinous streaks or knots, then wood primer	only under high gloss	1 or 2 coats solvent/oil-based or water-based gloss or satin finish
Bare hardwood	wood primer	only under high gloss	1 or 2 coats solvent/oil-based or water-based gloss or satin finish
Sound, painted wood	not needed	only under high gloss	1 or 2 coats solvent/oil-based or water-based gloss or satin finish
Metal			
New galvanized iron (some window frames for example)	quick-drying metal primer (or calcium plumbate – contains lead)	needed	1 or 2 coats of solvent/oil-based paint
Radiators (do not paint when hot)	quick-drying metal primer on bare metal	do not use undercoat	2 coats of solvent/oil-based paint

Choosing the right paint

Type	Uses	Advantages	Watchpoints
PRIMER Types include: all-purpose, wood, quick-drying metal, (calcium plumbate, alkali resisting)	Essential on new wood and metal. All-purpose primer is suitable for most surfaces around the home. Other primers are available for specific uses.	Seals the surface and provides a key for the next coat but bear in mind primer on its own does not give permanent protection – cover with undercoat and topcoat as quickly as possible.	Solvent/oil-based: clean brushes and thin with white (mineral) spirit. Water-based: use water for cleaning and thinning.
UNDERCOAT	Use after primer when building up a paint system on new wood or metal, or on old paintwork when changing colour significantly. (Not always necessary under one-coat paints)	Designed to have good covering power; can easily be rubbed smooth ready for a top coat. Undercoat, like primer, must be covered as quickly as possible.	Solvent/oil-based: clean brushes and thin with white (mineral) spirit. Water-based: use water for cleaning and thinning.

WATER-BASED PAINTS

Type	Uses	Advantages	Watchpoints
Matt vinyl emulsion/ Flat latex	For walls and ceilings. Being water-based they allow surface to breathe so use on new plaster or porous surfaces such as rough brickwork.	Covers well; reflects little light so will not highlight imperfections on uneven walls. Cheap, easy to apply, fast drying (recoatable in about 4 hours) and washable. Non-drip solid emulsion is ideal for ceilings.	Clean brushes and thin with water. Shows scuff marks and is likely to develop sheen with washing so best used in areas of light wear such as bedrooms, living rooms, dining rooms.
Silk vinyl emulsion/ Satin latex Soft sheen	For walls and ceilings – as for matt vinyl emulsion/flat latex	Tougher and more washable than above. Particularly effective on relief papers and other textured wallcoverings. Cheap, easy to apply, fast-drying (recoatable in about 4 hours). Non-drip solid emulsion is ideal for ceilings.	Clean brushes and thin with water. Will highlight irregular surfaces.
Kitchen and bathroom paint	For walls and ceilings	Moisture resistant formula that also contains a fungicide to stop mould growth. The satin finish contains a high percentage of acrylic, making it easy to wipe down.	Clean brushes and thin with water. Will highlight irregular surfaces.
Textured paint	For walls and ceilings	Gives a rough-stone finish which is good for disguising imperfect walls.	Clean brushes and thin with water. Difficult to wash.
Gloss/ Semi-gloss Satin finish	Interior woodwork	Easier to apply than solvent/oil-based gloss . Recoatable in about 6 hours.	Clean brushes and thin with water. Gloss not as shiny as solvent/oil-based.

SOLVENT/OIL-BASED PAINTS

Type	Uses	Advantages	Watchpoints
Satin/flat finish	All-purpose paint for walls and ceilings, wood and metal. Ideal for areas of heavy condensation such as kitchens and bathrooms.	Tougher than emulsion (latex) and more subtle than gloss. Wears well and is washable. Normally needs no undercoat (though bare surfaces should be primed) and needs less brushing out than most gloss.	Clean brushes and thin with white (mineral) spirit. More expensive than emulsion (latex). Takes 12-16 hours to dry and needs more careful application than emulsion (latex).
Gloss/high gloss one-coat non-drip liquid	For surfaces that need maximum protection – kitchen cupboards, window sills and other woodwork.	Easy to clean and hardwearing. *One-coat* formula needs no undercoat. *Non-drip* needs no stirring and there's less chance of splashes and runs than with liquid gloss. Applied quite thickly, which means fewer coats and good covering power. *Liquid gloss* flows on evenly and is particularly good for difficult surfaces such as window frames and mouldings.	Clean brushes and thin with white (mineral) spirit.Takes 12-16 hours to dry. The shiny finish highlights surface flaws so thorough preparation is necessary. Liquid gloss is slightly cheaper than one-coat, but is more difficult to use and needs an undercoat.

Painting equipment

Choose the right tool – brush, roller or pad – for all your painting jobs.

Whatever you are painting, you want to use a tool which puts the paint on smoothly and easily with the minimum of surface blemishes. A brush is the traditional tool to use, but in some situations a roller or a paint pad could be a better choice.

Paint brushes

The familiar general purpose paint brush consists of a wedge of bristles secured in a block of synthetic resin and bound to a wooden or plastic handle by a metal ferrule.

Brushes made of natural bristle are best used for applying solvent/oil-based paints. Their natural split ends not only hold paint well, but also help to apply it smoothly and leave a fine surface finish.

Synthetic bristle brushes are available for applying the more user friendly water-based paints which are becoming increasingly popular. The bristle absorbs little water so maintains a constant performance.

Special brushes are also made for applying emulsion (latex) paint, for stains and preservatives, for varnish and for masonry paints.

Buying brushes

Good-quality brushes have more and longer bristles than cheaper versions, so they hold more paint and brush it out more evenly. They also tend to shed bristles less often and generally last longer. Buy good brushes if you decorate regularly and are prepared to clean and store them carefully. Where the quality of finish does not matter, use cheaper brushes and throw them away afterwards, or use them for other jobs like applying paint stripper.

Brush sizes

Paint brushes are available in a range of sizes. The commonest are 12, 18, 25, 50, 75, 100mm (½, ¾, 1, 2, 3, 4in) wide. Emulsion (latex) brushes and masonry brushes come in larger sizes – 125mm (5in) and 150mm (6in). These are useful if you have an expanse of wall to paint and help you to cover the area faster.

Small paint brushes with bristles cut off at an angle – called cutting-in brushes – are used when painting into an internal angle. This makes it easier to keep the paint off the adjoining surface. You can also get special brushes with extended handles for painting behind radiators and the back of downpipes.

Where to use

A brush is more versatile than a roller or paint pad, since its bristles can reach easily into all sorts of awkward corners and crevices.

Use a small brush for painting narrow surfaces such as panel mouldings, a cutting-in brush for window glazing bars and similar angled surfaces, and a wide brush on flat, uninterrupted surfaces such as flush doors, walls and ceilings. Use a wide brush for painting over heavily textured surfaces too. As a rule, the bigger the brush the quicker the work proceeds. However, a wide brush can be tiring to use, especially with thicker solvent paints.

natural bristle brush

wall brush

cutting-in brush

radiator brush

paint guard

Paint pads

A paint pad consists of a piece of short-pile fabric stuck to a foam backing pad which is attached to a plastic or metal handle. To use one, dip the pile into the paint held in a shallow container or a special loading tray and then draw it across the surface to deposit and spread out the paint. Paint pads tend to put on a thinner film than a brush or roller does, which may mean that you have to apply two coats to get adequate coverage.

Buying paint pads

Most paint pads are sold in sets, but you can buy them individually if you have only a small area to paint. When you buy one or more, it is a good idea to stock up on refill pads for the brand concerned, since they are not interchangeable between brands.

The container in which paint pads are sold usually doubles as a paint tray, but specially designed trays are also available separately.

Pad sizes

Paint pads come in sizes, from large wall pads measuring up to 200 x 100mm (8 x 4in) to small wands for painting narrow surfaces such as mouldings. Some pads have guide wheels along one edge, making it easier to paint up to edges like glass. Pads for corners and moulded or rough surfaces are also available.

Where to use

Paint pads work best on flat surfaces, and many people prefer them to brushes or rollers in this situation. You need to switch from a flat pad to a speciality pad for more fiddly jobs like painting into corners. You can use paint pads with solvent-based paints as well as water-based ones, although the solvents may cause the pads to deteriorate quite quickly.

pad set with tray

wand

edging pad

Paint rollers

A paint roller consists of a rigid tubular sleeve which fits over a rotating cage attached to a handle, allowing you to push the roller backwards and forwards over the surface you are decorating. Most rollers have a single arm linking the cage to the handle, enabling them to paint reasonably close to internal corners; double-arm versions are available and are easier to use when fitted with an extension pole for decorating ceilings.

The cheapest sleeves are just cylinders of plastic foam sponge, and are not recommended because they absorb a lot of paint and are splashy to use. Fibre sleeves give much better results. They have either a natural sheepskin, lambswool or wool pile or a synthetic pile, which may be short, medium or long.

roller tray

sponge roller

pile roller

radiator roller

extension pole

Buying rollers and sleeves

Good-quality sleeves last longer than cheap ones, which tend to peel away from their cores in time. Check that they are a tight fit over the cage, and that the roller arm between cage and handle is rigid enough not to deform during use.

For applying emulsion (latex) and other water-based paints, the pile type is less important than choosing the right pile length – short for flat surfaces, medium for anything with a slight surface texture and long for heavily embossed surfaces such as relief wallcoverings. For solvent/oil-based paints on flat surfaces use a short-pile mohair roller.

Moulded sleeves with different raised patterns are excellent for applying a variety of textured paint finishes to walls and ceilings.

You have to buy a roller tray to match the size of the roller you are using.

Roller sizes

The commonest roller and sleeve size is 175mm (7in) wide, but 225 and 300mm (9 and 12in) sizes are also made. Sleeves generally fit any brand of roller, and are easy to replace.

There are also several narrower rollers for getting into awkward and confined spaces. *Radiator rollers* have a narrow sleeve and long handle for painting the walls behind radiators. *Pipe rollers* have two small sleeves that straddle the pipe. *Narrow rollers* are designed for painting along skirting boards.

Where to use

A roller is the best choice for painting large flat wall and ceiling surfaces that have no obstructions, since you have to load it with paint less often than a brush or a pad and you can cover a large area quite quickly.

However, you still have to use a brush or pad to paint edges, corners, intricate mouldings and other fiddly areas that the roller cannot reach.

Both short and long extension poles are available for getting to the tops of walls and painting ceilings without using a stepladder.

Useful accessories

Pour a small amount of paint into a *paint kettle* if the paint can is very large or if you are using a stepladder. A kettle is also useful for mixing or thinning paint. You can hang it from a ladder with an S-hook.

A *paint guard* keeps paint off the adjoining area and stops the brush picking up debris from dusty surfaces. Some guards have sucker pads to stick them to the glass, which leaves one hand free for you to do the actual painting. An *opener* for prising off the lid of the can and a *paint stirrer* are also useful.

Care and maintenance

The secret of keeping painting tools in good condition is to clean them very thoroughly after use – with soapy water for emulsion (latex) paints and other water-based types, and with white (mineral) spirit or proprietary brush cleaner followed by soapy water for solvent/oil-based paints. Check the instructions on the paint tin to see which solvent to use.

Cleaning brushes

Remove excess paint from the brush with the back of a knife, scraping the bristles from ferrule to tip. For water-based paints, rinse the brush under running water; for solvent/oil-based types, half fill a jam jar with white (mineral) spirit or brush cleaner and agitate the brush so that the liquid gets into the bristles. In both cases, finish by washing with warm soapy water, using your fingers to work the soap into the bristles. Finally rinse the brush under running water. Shake and dry with a lint-free rag. Wrap the brush in paper and store it flat.

Cleaning rollers

Roll out excess paint on newspaper or run a special circular scraper along the sleeve. For water-based paints, hold the sleeve under running water until clean; for solvent/oil-based paints, work white (mineral) spirit or brush cleaner into the pile, then wash in soapy water and rinse. To store, wrap the sleeve in paper and hang it on its frame.

Cleaning pads

Clean paint pads like paint rollers. Do not leave pad to soak in solvent or hot water. Store it in its container, pile up.

Care in use

Clean the applicator every two or three hours to prevent a build-up of dried paint. If you stop in mid-session, wrap it in foil or plastic film to keep it moist.

Painting techniques

Find out how to apply paint to a surface correctly – the essential skill in getting the best result.

The technique you use for painting depends on three things:
❖ the tool you are using – brush, roller or pad.
❖ the type of paint you are using – in particular, how quickly it dries.
❖ the surface you are painting – its area and texture.

In many painting tasks you need to keep what professional decorators term a wet edge. As implied, it is the edge of the area you have just painted where the paint is still wet. This edge is used as the starting point for the next block of painting, so that the two areas blend inconspicuously. If the edge is allowed to dry, a visible, hardened ridge forms on the surface.

Before starting any painting job, buy at least enough paint to complete the first coat and make sure that all other surfaces within splashing range are protected by dust sheets or newspaper. Keep a clean rag and some brush cleaner handy in case of spills. Work in a clean room, in good light, from a safe, comfortable position.

Painting with a brush

A natural bristle brush is the traditional way of putting on gloss paint. For the main areas, use the largest size you feel comfortable with – say 50mm (2in) – but have a smaller one ready for the fiddly bits.

1 Using a new brush for the first time Before loading a new brush with paint, make sure you remove any loose or broken bristles by flicking it across your hand as though painting your palm.

2 Loading with paint Stir the paint (unless it is non-drip) and pour a little into a separate container. Dip the brush into the paint to cover the top third of the bristles and wipe off surplus on the edge of the container.

3 Brushing on the paint Holding the metal ferrule between your fingers and thumb, apply the paint over a small area of the surface in two or three vertical strips about 2.5cm (1in) apart. Brush across these at right angles to spread the paint evenly.

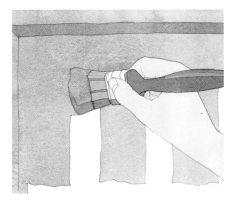

4 Laying off the paint Without re-loading the brush, finish off by painting light vertical strokes, brushing from the wet edge into the painted area so that you leave a thinner layer of paint along the sides. This is called laying off.

Using a brush for emulsion (latex) paint. Water-based emulsion paints dry more quickly than gloss paints, so you need to modify your painting technique. Paint round any edges with a small brush before starting on the main body of the wall or ceiling. For the main areas use a much larger brush and hold it in the palm of your hand rather than between your fingers. Apply the paint as quickly as possible, working in two directions and feathering the wet edges by brushing the paint away to nothing.

Painting along an edge

Lay the paint brush on its side, so the bristles follow a straight line – known as 'cutting in'. A special brush with angled bristles is available for painting very thin sections, such as window glazing bars.

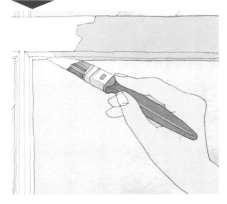

Using a roller

When it comes to painting walls and ceilings, most people choose to apply emulsion (latex) paint with a roller. You can't use a roller along edges, however, so you need to use a small paint brush to paint them before you start on the main expanse of wall or ceiling.

Be careful not to overload the roller to avoid spattering the area with excess paint.

Using a roller for gloss paint

Use a short-pile mohair roller for gloss paint; it is quicker than a brush, but not as quick as a pad, and it does tend to leave a slightly textured surface. Other types of roller are not suitable.

1 Using a roller for the first time Rinse a new roller thoroughly under the tap before using it, to make sure that you get rid of any loose bits of pile and dirt.

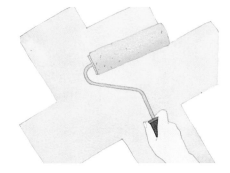

2 Loading the roller Load the roller by rolling it into a small amount of paint in the roller tray. Run the roller up and down the sloping surface of the tray to make sure that the paint is evenly spread throughout the pile. This ensures it does not drip.

3 Applying the paint Put the paint on the wall by drawing out a W or X shape. Then pass the roller across both horizontally and vertically so that the paint is spread evenly. On rough surfaces, be sure to work the paint into all the hollows.

Using a paint pad

A paint pad is ideal for putting on gloss paint, as it can spread paint more evenly than a paint brush. For flat areas, use the largest size you can comfortably hold; use a smaller pad on the mouldings of a panel door or the glazing bars of a window.

Using a paint pad for emulsion

(latex): Large pads, which are often fitted with extension handles, are used for walls and ceilings. The technique is similar to using a smaller paint pad for gloss paint – apply the paint in long smooth strokes until the pad is empty. Because the paint goes on more thinly than with a brush or a roller, you may need an extra coat, especially if you are covering a dark colour with a lighter one. Use a scrubbing action on rough or textured surfaces to work the paint into hollows.

1 Using a new pad for the first time To avoid the tiny mohair bristles falling out, give a new pad a good clean in soapy water and then let it dry. Rub your hand roughly across the surface to make sure there are no loose bristles.

2 Loading with paint Partially fill the special paint pad tray with paint. Make sure that only the bristles are allowed to touch the paint – do not allow any paint to get into the foam backing – and wipe off excess paint on the side of the tray.

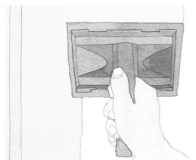

3 Applying the paint Paint the surface in adjacent vertical strips, the width of the paint pad, until it runs out of paint. Because the technique is so fast and the paint spreads very evenly, you don't need to worry about keeping a wet edge.

A    B   C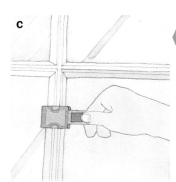

Painting an edge
There are speciality pads for awkward jobs:
(**A**) Some pads have wheels for painting right up to edges.
(**B**) Flexible pads are ideal for painting corners or edges.
(**C**) Small wands are handy for painting window frames.

Correcting faulty paintwork

Imperfections in the painted finish do happen, so it is worth knowing how to remedy them. Understanding the causes of painting faults also helps you to avoid them in the first place. Where the recommended remedy is to rub down and repaint, you should leave the surface to harden for at least a week before working on it.

Defect	Cause	Remedy
Runs, sags, tears	Paint applied too thickly or not laid off	Lay off if wet, otherwise allow to dry completely, rub down and repaint
Flaking	Poor surface preparation	Rub down, fill and repaint – or strip surface and start again
Blistering	Usually damp timber	Prick blisters to allow water to escape, rub down and repaint
Crazing (orange peel)	Incompatible paints	Rub down, fill and repaint or strip surface and start again
Wrinkles	Paint applied before previous coat has dried	Strip surface and start again
Grainy surface	Usually dust in the drying paint	Rub down and repaint
Brush marks	Poor quality brush, or insufficiently sanded surface underneath	Rub down thoroughly and repaint

STAMP DECORATIONS

Rubber stamping is a simple and effective way of decorating almost any flat surface. It only takes a few seconds to print one motif, and a couple of hours to cover a large wall.

For centuries people have been using printing stamps to decorate plain walls and floors in every type of dwelling – from humble cottages to palaces and monasteries. Recently interior designers have rediscovered the art of stamping as a quick, easy way of printing small motifs on wood, plaster, glass and fabric.

Today, the stamps are made from synthetic rubber instead of wood, and you can buy them from stationery shops, art and craft shops and specialist mail order companies. As you apply stamps by hand, the blocks are generally no larger than 10cm (4in) square and consist of simple, clearly defined outlines such as hearts or stars.

The basic technique requires no special skills – coat the stamp in paint, using either a roller or an inkpad and then press it down firmly on to a flat surface to leave an impression.

You can print a single motif in a couple of seconds, and it need only take an hour to repeat the same motif hundreds of times across a wall, as an economical alternative to wallpaper. Because you can apply the stamp one-handed and the paint is touch dry almost immediately, it is an ideal way of decorating awkward areas such as a ceiling or stairwell without performing dangerous balancing acts or ducking paint drips.

As with any new decorating technique, it is worth experimenting with design ideas on paper before you start stamping everything in sight. The delight of stamping is that once you have mastered the basic technique, the creative possibilities are endless.

A pattern of tiny hearts repeatedly stamped across a roughly colourwashed wall gives this kitchen an appealing country feel.

TYPES OF PAINT

Walls and ceilings Use emulsion (latex) or acrylic paint for printing. If you make a mistake on an emulsion-painted surface allow the motif to dry, then paint over with the base colour and start again.

Wooden surfaces It is possible to use gloss paint to print, but you will find it far easier to use an acrylic or a suitable water-based craft paint. The surface must be free from grease or wax. Sand off any mistakes with fine sandpaper. Seal the finished work with one or two coats of polyurethane varnish.

Fabric and ceramics Use the appropriate craft paint for the material you are printing. Check the manufacturer's instructions for applying and fixing the paint before starting.

▼ *Stamp-printing a plain wall with regularly spaced motifs recreates the look of wallpaper. To copy this look you need to measure and mark the wall lightly in pencil before you start. The pencil marks will be hidden by the paint.*

ROLLER METHOD

 Coating the roller Pour a small amount of paint into a shallow container. Roll it out with the roller to form a thin, even layer on the base of the container. Do not be tempted to pour in lots of paint – it clogs up the roller, which then applies too much paint to the stamp, making the print look smudgy.

Applying the paint to the stamp Prime the roller with paint from the container and roll it evenly over the raised stamp.

Stamping the design Press the stamp firmly against the surface you are decorating and hold it there for a few seconds. Recoat the stamp with paint before printing each impression. When the design is complete, wash the stamp, roller and dish in water or the appropriate solvent .

COLOUR TECHNIQUES

INKPAD METHOD

You normally print with a stamp in just one colour, but you can get some interesting multi-coloured effects by merging two colours to form a third as shown below. The basic rules of colour mixing apply: red + yellow = orange, red + blue = purple, yellow + blue = green.

You can buy coloured inkpads, and dry inkpads to use with any paint you like. To fill a dry inkpad, pour a little paint on the surface and let it soak in for a few seconds. Test stamp on a sheet of scrap paper and add extra paint a little at a time until the pad is moist but not flooded with paint. Dab the stamp on the pad to coat it with paint before stamping each motif. Clean the pad thoroughly after use and allow it to dry.

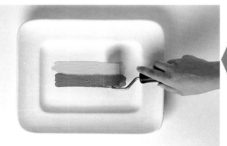

Roller stripes For the best results, use stiff acrylic paint. Squeeze a little of each colour side by side at one end of the mixing tray. Roll out the paint firmly, in one direction only, so the two colours merge in the centre to form a third colour. Apply the paint to the stamp, rolling in one direction only.

Inkpad merge Pour a little of the first colour in the centre of the pad, and then pour a ring of the second colour around it. As the paint soaks into the pad, the two colours merge to form a third.

◁ *Armed with a little paint, a well-primed inkpad and a few rubber stamps you can create a great variety of designs on walls, furniture, fabric and ceramics.*

PRINT EFFECTS

Rubber stamps are amazingly versatile tools to have in your decorating kit. They are especially useful for creating some instant coordinating effects between walls and fabric, fabrics and furniture or walls and accessories. It is much less expensive – and often far more effective – to paint walls in a single colour or to buy plain fabrics and to stamp on your own, original patterns. If you plan the arrangement of the motifs before you start printing, you can create some highly regular designs or print borders and surrounds. Otherwise, you can apply the stamp haphazardly over part or all of the surface.

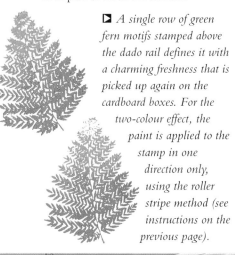

▶ *A single row of green fern motifs stamped above the dado rail defines it with a charming freshness that is picked up again on the cardboard boxes. For the two-colour effect, the paint is applied to the stamp in one direction only, using the roller stripe method (see instructions on the previous page).*

▲ *A stamped pattern can look just as pretty as wallpaper and doesn't take any longer to apply. You can also print the same daisy motif on matching curtains and cushions.*

▶ *Stars stamped at random across the walls and repeated inside the cabinet and on the curtains give this living room an interesting mock-Gothic look.*

SIMPLE STENCILLING

*Stencilling is an inexpensive but highly effective
way of enhancing or even transforming the look of a room,
and a simple technique that anyone can learn.*

P lain walls, furniture, floors, soft furnishings and household accessories – all can be stencilled to create whatever look you want, be it romantic, country farmhouse, chic or simply fun. You can choose motif designs either to contrast with or to match background furnishings and decorations. And by using the same motifs on walls and furniture, you can link them for an overall effect. You can also match theme to function, for example by stencilling aquatic motifs in the bathroom.

Sometimes just a few strategically placed motifs are all you need, so think carefully about what the finished result will be before you start. This way you avoid the risk of making the room appear busy with too many elaborate motifs.

Stencilling is not a difficult technique to learn. Begin with straightforward, single colour designs before progressing to more complicated multi-coloured ones. Once you have mastered the basics you can go on to create your own unique designs for a truly individual effect.

Repeating a single colour motif elegantly enhances a plain background. Here a simple white design is repeated to break up and brighten the dark green wall.

▶ **Butterflies and dragonflies** take flight as dainty stencilled decorations for these small paper lampshades. When stencilling round a curve, check the stencil is pressed well down on the surface.

▲ **Less is more** – this stylish fleur-de-lys motif adds a touch of regal class to the cabinet. Its gold colouring is a rich complement to the deep red of the painted wood.

▶ **Simple stencils** can transform otherwise ordinary household accessories. This delicate green trail-of-ivy motif brings a flourish of life to a bare white tray.

▲ **Imaginative motifs** like these delightful angel fish, sea shells and duck designs decorate a set of storage boxes with cheerful colour.

◀ **Stencilling can be fun,** as in the case of this train motif in a child's bedroom. Keep the colours bold and bright and the designs simple.

Ready-cut stencils

A quick way of producing a decorative motif, stencilling couldn't be easier to do.

With stencilling, colour is brushed, sponged or sprayed over a cut-out shape. It's a simple and flexible technique that allows you to apply your own choice of paint in your chosen colour scheme to a given stencil design. For simplicity, pre-cut stencils are available in designs ranging from small single motifs to large, intricate border patterns. For the more detailed designs you build up the effect using separate stencil sheets for each colour.

Stencilling can be used to decorate most surfaces, including walls, woodwork, floors and ceilings, furniture, fabric and ceramics. Work on matt or satin surfaces for the best results. The surface to be stencilled should be clean, sound and smooth. Lightly sand over bare wood, paint and varnish to key the surface; wipe china and tiles with methylated spirit (denatured alcohol) to remove all grease.

The most common type of ready-cut stencil is made of clear plastic film, which is easy to position and bends round curved surfaces. Oiled or waxed card or metal stencils are also available.

Stencils, brushes and paints are sold in DIY and home decorating stores and art shops.

Paints for stencilling

Wherever possible use a thick, quick drying paint, which is less likely to seep underneath the stencil and give a messy edge to your motif.

Stencil paints (water based) are thick, dry almost instantly, and can be used on most walls, ceilings, natural wood/painted furniture and unglazed ceramics e.g. terracotta, that's kept indoors. They're not suitable for glazed surfaces.

Stencil sticks (oil based) produce good rich colours. Shading is easier than with paint, but allow plenty of drying time. Like stencil paints, they can be used on most matt surfaces.

Vinyl emulsion/latex (water based) is easy to use and fast drying. Small test pots are ideal. Can be used on most matt surfaces.

Wood stains (solvent/oil based) in interior and exterior grades can be used to stencil patterns on bare wooden furniture and floors in colours that tint the wood, allowing the grain to show through.

Masonry paints (water based) provide a weatherproof finish on unglazed ceramics such as terracotta for outdoors.

Textile paints are designed for use on fabrics. Some become permanent on drying, others are heat-set with an iron. Use natural fibre fabrics for the best results; synthetic fabrics tend to resist the paint. Leave stencilled fabrics for two weeks before washing.

Enamel polymer paints (solvent/oil-based) for glazed tiles and china. Best for small, unfixed items that can be baked in your oven after stencilling, though you can use a hairdrier on fixed tiles. They will withstand a degree of bathroom wear.

Cold ceramic paints (solvent/oil-based) dry in 24 hours and should then be varnished. Use them on tiles and decorative glazed ceramic pottery. They're not suitable for constantly wet and steamy areas such as around a shower. Stencilled ceramic ware is not dishwasher safe.

Spray paints (solvent/oil based) are suitable for most surfaces, including tiles (but not steamy bathrooms); they're good for rough finishes such as wicker and matting. Take small items outside to stencil, or work in a well ventilated room; protect the surrounding area with newspaper.

Other materials

Stencil brushes have short stiff bristles which are cut bluntly across the end to give a softly stippled finish.

Synthetic or natural sponges add a dappled look.

Masking tape holds the stencil in place; for an intricate design needing precise paint application use a spray mounting adhesive in a well ventilated room.

Craft knife

Paint

Card stencil

Stencil brushes

Metal stencil

Sponge

Stencil brush

Plastic stencil

Stencilling techniques

For a successful result, experiment first on a sheet of scrap paper to master the technique, and explore the various effects you can achieve with the different paints and methods of application.

To create interest and subtle shading on single colour areas, apply the paint lightly at first. Then build up more colour in discrete places by going over the same area several times. Using darker and lighter shades of the same colour will form regions of shadows and highlights. Always make sure the paint is dry before removing or repositioning the stencil.

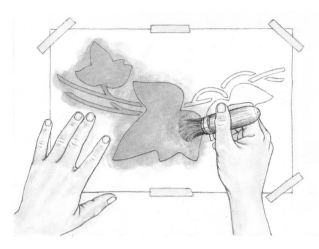

Using a brush Dip the tip of the brush into the paint and remove excess on scrap paper. The brush should be almost dry. Hold the brush at right angles to the surface and dab the paint into the cut-out areas, working in an up and down or circular motion from the outside towards the centre.

Using a sponge Slightly dampen the sponge. Pour a small amount of paint into a saucer, press a corner of the sponge into it, then dab off the paint on scrap paper until the sponge is nearly dry. Lightly dab the sponge on to the cut-out areas.

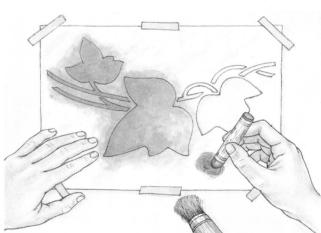

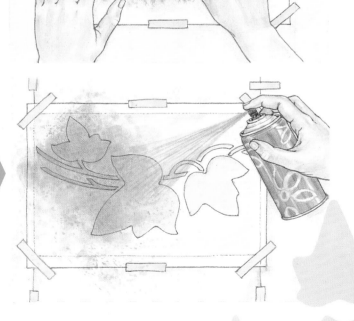

Using a stencil stick Rub some colour from the stick on to an uncut piece of the stencil. Work the colour into the bristles of a brush in a circular motion. Use the brush to work the colour over the cut-out shape, moving in a circular motion from the outside towards the centre.

Using spray paint Work outside or in a well ventilated room and mask off surrounding areas. Shake the can well and make sure the stencil is held tightly in place. Build up the colour gradually by spraying on several fine coats of paint.

Protecting designs

When the paint is completely dry, seal stencilled surfaces that are subject to wear with gloss or matt polyurethane varnish. Apply two or three coats – or more on areas such as floorboards – gently sanding down between each one. Varnished surfaces can just be wiped over to clean.

Cleaning stencils and brushes

Clean card stencils with a paper towel or rag dipped in water for water-based paints, white (mineral) spirit for solvent/oil-based products. Rinse plastic stencils under the tap or wipe over with white spirit. Store stencils flat, separated by sheets of newspaper. Wash stencil brushes with appropriate cleaner and bind bristles with paper held in place with an elastic band.

RANDOM STENCILLING

Break up a plain surface with scattered stencilled motifs in two or more colours, or group them together to form larger designs for extra impact.

Using a single stencil you can create a variety of original decorative effects on a wall. Unlike a stencil border that forms a continuous repeat pattern along a wall, a single stencil motif either stands on its own as a complete decoration or can be repeated at random as many times as you like, in as many places as you want, to create a pattern. With one little butterfly you can print a cloud of beautiful butterflies.

The motif may be a delicate spray of flowers, carefully positioned to highlight a feature such as an arch in a room, or a group of cheerful teddy bears to add colour and excitement to a corner in a child's bedroom. Single motifs printed all over the wall, and edged with a stencil border, look just as attractive as a wallpaper and its matching border, and cost half the price.

As with any type of stencil, you can pick out small details of the design and stencil them independently on to pieces of furniture and other accessories for a fully coordinated look to the entire room.

A sage-green bow and ribbon design provides an elegant heading for a dried flower wreath. For a design with a stronger impact, you could paint the flanking ribbons in another colour. Examples of mixed colour stencils follow.

MULTI-SHEET STENCILLING

Instead of masking off the areas of the design to be painted in different colours, multi-sheet stencilling calls for a separate cut stencil sheet for each colour. In order to position every colour accurately, you must line up each stencil sheet precisely on top of the part of the design that is already printed – this is known as the registration. Generally, it's best to print the lightest colour first and the darkest one last of all, so use the sheets in that order.

REGISTRATION METHODS

The registration method depends on whether the stencils are made from clear acetate or manila card. Read the registration instructions on the pack carefully before you start stencilling.

Acetate stencils are the easiest to use because they are transparent. The entire design is visible through the stencil sheets, even when you are colouring a different area of the design. Each stencil sheet usually has the outline of the rest of the colours in the motif printed on it so that it's easy to line them up with the sections of the design that you have already stencilled.

Card stencils have a V-shaped notch cut off the top and bottom edges, or holes pierced in the four corners. These are called *registration marks*. When the first stencil is in position, mark the notches or holes on the wall with a pencil. Line up the notches or holes on the subsequent stencil sheets with these marks for perfect registration.

POSITIONING THE MOTIF

To test the position of the stencil motif on the wall, stencil a piece of scrap paper first. Then cut out this paper motif and attach it to the wall with masking tape. Stand back to view the effect, and then reposition the paper design as many times as you like until you are satisfied with the result. Lightly mark the position for the stencil in a soft pencil on the wall by drawing round the test motif and remove the piece of paper.

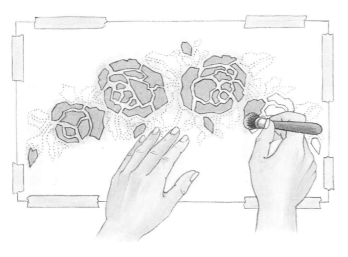

1 **Positioning the first stencil** Fix the stencil sheet for the first colour in position on the wall with masking tape or spray adhesive. Apply the paint with a light dabbing motion, and leave to dry. Carefully remove the stencil.

2 **Using the next stencil** Place the stencil for the second colour over the stencilled first colour. Check that the stencil is correctly registered, and secure in place as before. Apply the second colour and leave to dry.

3 **Printing further colours** Register and print any remaining colours in the same way. Always check that the paint is completely dry before printing another colour, otherwise the design may smudge.

◁ *A large rose and leaf stencil frames a picture. The colours of the stencil echo the soft watercolours of the print.*

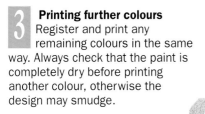

◁ *A stencilled design of trailing honeysuckle in three colours frames the top corner of a bathroom shelf. Using spray paint for the stencil produces a soft, diffused look.*

STENCILLED DETAILS

Stencilling works effectively on a wide range of wall surfaces, from plain painted walls, wallpaper and painted brickwork to wooden tongue-and-groove or dado panelling – it just depends on the decorative look you want.

Almost any room in your home gets a new lease of life from a stencilled design or two, arranged in formal patterns or apparently at random. Another advantage of a stencil is that it instantly personalizes anything it adorns.

A benefit of stencil designs is their complete flexibility. There is an almost limitless supply of motifs, and even if you don't find exactly what you want in kit form, you can always originate your own stencils or copy a design from a book or magazine. Stencilling works equally well in elegant formal surroundings, such as drawing rooms as in bright informal playrooms – you can be as subtle as you want, or as bold as you dare.

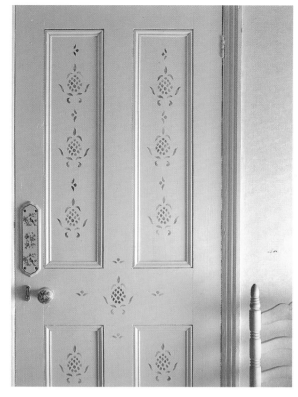

▲ *An abstract stencil design in soft red and green positioned on the panels of an internal door complements the ceramic door knob and door plate.*

▼ *A bedroom decorated in pretty blue and cream floral fabric looks even more romantic with the addition of bird and flower stencils positioned randomly on cream-washed walls.*

▲ *This elegant white fitted bedroom has a crisp clean look. The stencilled vase of flowers and the tulips either side add a stylish finishing touch.*

▶ *Stencils can be used in the most surprising places – here a heart-inspired floral motif draws attention to an attractive brass light fitting.*

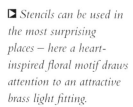

STENCILLING A BORDER

A stencilled room has a charm all of its own. Follow this simple guide to stencilling attractive and effective borders, and enhance the look of your home.

A s well as looking very appealing, a stencilled border can have an architectural impact, in the same way as a wallpaper border. It can highlight existing features such as arches and fireplaces, and make featureless interiors more interesting. In a room with bare walls, a stencilled border can add character and subtly alter the proportions of the room, making it look more elegant, or cosier.

A stencilled border can be used at skirting board, dado or picture rail level, or immediately below the ceiling to make it seem lower. Around windows and doors a stencilled border frames and decorates in the same way as a wallpaper border, but with a more individual character.

Also, of course, any part of a border stencil can be picked out and reproduced as a separate motif on items of furniture and accessories, for a coordinated room colour and pattern scheme.

A stencilled border can be continuous or non-continuous. A continuous border is a line of motifs repeated without any breaks. Usually the stencil is self-overlapping, and made from clear acetate so that you can easily register the overlaps.

A non-continuous border is a line of repeated but separate motifs and is made with a stand-alone stencil. The stencil can be made of acetate or card; acetate is often easier to use as it is flexible and transparent.

Stencilling a border isn't difficult if you use a pre-cut stencil. It's also worth paying a little extra for proper stencil paint when stencilling a border; its quick drying properties allow you to work steadily around the room without having to keep stopping to wait for it to dry.

Real shells, coral and a sea sponge are a perfect complement to the marine theme of this stencilled bathroom wall. The pattern incorporates a border of shells, with the motifs neatly reversed.

PLANNING THE BORDER

Careful planning is the key to a successful stencilled border. First decide on the position of the border. If you put it immediately above or below a dado or picture rail, or at ceiling height or skirting board level, you have a ready line to guide you. Otherwise, use a level to find the true horizontal, and lightly pencil a dotted line all the way around the wall to mark the top or bottom of the stencil, as appropriate.

> ### YOU WILL NEED
> ❖ STENCILS
> ❖ STENCIL PAINTS and BRUSHES
> ❖ (SPIRIT) LEVEL
> ❖ STEEL TAPE
> ❖ SET SQUARE/TRIANGLE
> ❖ MASKING TAPE

CONTINUOUS STENCILLING

With a continuous border, start by marking the mid point of the most eye-catching section of wall. Centre the first stencil above or below this mark as appropriate, then work away from it in both directions.

You can continue some designs straight around corners without a break – bend the stencil around the corner and hold it firmly in place while you apply the paint. With other designs it is best to stop when you reach a corner, then start again from the centre of the next section of wall. When this is the case, always lengthen rather than shorten the design if it doesn't fit into the corner exactly – a shortened design always looks wrong. In all cases, because walls are rarely absolutely straight or corners at true angles, make slight adjustments by eye to keep the border on line.

When the design calls for more than one colour, a separate stencil for each colour is usually supplied, with only the relevant parts cut out on each, so there is no need for masking. Apply one colour at a time, working all the way around the room before starting with the next colour. Wait until you have finished the border and all the paint has dried before erasing pencil marks.

◪ *A continuous stencil such as this attractive pear border can be run vertically or horizontally.*

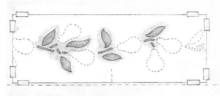

1 **Positioning the first stencil** Centre the first stencil at the mid point of the wall, aligning it with the horizontal, and secure all round the edges with small strips of tape. Apply the paint, and leave to dry.

2 **Continuing the design** Carefully peel the stencil off the wall, keeping the tape intact. Reposition the stencil so that the pattern overlaps exactly. Apply the paint as before. Continue along the wall, then repeat for each separate colour until the whole border design is complete.

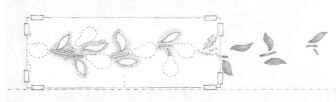

For a continuous stencilled border around a door, window or fireplace, you need to pivot the design to negotiate right angled bends. There are four ways of doing this.

Butting With simple, evenly spaced designs, simply work out the best point to break off, and continue the stencil vertically, either above or below it.

Trailing With a flowing, floral type of design you can curve it gently around a right angle. Practise on paper first. You might have to omit or add a few elements from the design.

Using corner motifs Many stencil designs contain an element that can be extracted as a corner motif. Alternatively, you can use a separate stencil – specially designed corner motifs are available.

Mitring Geometric designs can be mitred at right angled bends. Try mitring other designs for a professional looking finish.

MITRING CORNERS

1 Marking the angle Using a set square (triangle), draw a line at 45° to bisect the right angle. Place tape along the line.

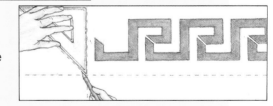

2 Stencilling along the horizontal Stencil along the horizontal, taking the paint up to the edge of the tape. Leave to dry.

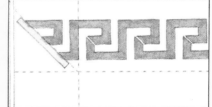

3 Stencilling the vertical Reposition the tape on the other side of the diagonal line. Stencil along the vertical, taking the paint up to the edge of the tape. Wait until all the paint has completely dried before removing the tape and rubbing out any pencil lines.

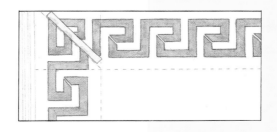

▲ *An effective stencilled border blends in with the existing decorations, drawing the eye without being too obvious — as with these pretty pastel patterns running discreetly up beside the door and along the top of the dado rail.*

59

Non-continuous Stencilling

A non-continuous border looks best when each section of wall comprises whole stencils only, so work on each section separately. The stencils must be evenly spaced. A bold design on a small section of wall usually looks best when there is a stencil centred over the mid point.

To position the stencils evenly in a row, use a piece of chalk to mark off the length of each stencil, plus the spaces between. You might have to adjust the spacing slightly to accommodate the pattern at the corners.

Apply one colour at a time all around the wall. If only one stencil is supplied, use tape to mask off the cutout parts that you don't want to paint in a particular colour.

1 Centring the first stencil Lightly mark the mid point of the wall. Centre the first stencil at this point and mark the corners of the stencil in pencil.

2 Marking the repeats Lightly mark the position of each stencil on the wall, leaving the space you have worked out between each stencil.

▲ *Simple, bold, single colour motifs work just as well as intricate border designs, especially on a plain background. Here the border on the wall is cleverly repeated on an old trunk.*

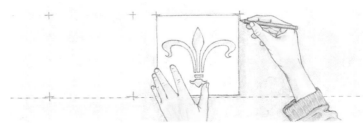

3 Applying the paint In a multi-coloured design, apply one colour at a time, working your way round the wall before returning to the start and applying the next colour, using the pencilled corner marks as registration guides. Wait until all the paint has dried before rubbing out pencil marks.

☑ *Gold paint over a deep blue background gives wonderful richness to a stylish non-continuous fleur-de-lis stencil.*

▼▼▼▼▼ **T I P** ▼▼▼▼▼

SPRAY MOUNT
A quick and easy alternative to masking tape for sticking stencils to a wall is low tack spray adhesive, which is readily available from art and craft shops. Simply lay the stencil face down on a sheet of newspaper and spray it all over. The stencil will then stick to the wall but will peel off easily when you want to move it.

▲▲▲▲▲▲▲▲▲▲▲▲▲

EMBOSSED WALLCOVERINGS

Add distinction to your walls with an embossed wallcovering and enhance the look of your room. There are ranges to suit all styles, whether it's elegantly Edwardian, quietly classic or stylishly modern.

One of the most original and satisfying ways of giving an impressive finish to your walls or ceilings is to use a wallcovering with a raised pattern. Often called white embossed because they are designed to be painted after hanging, these relief wallcoverings come in a range of high or low relief patterns in a variety of styles, including classic, Edwardian, Colonial, rural and modern geometric designs.

Painted embossed wallcoverings provide a tough, durable finish – traditionally the heavier types were used to withstand knocks below the dado rail in a hall, and this is still a favoured position for wallcoverings such as Lincrusta. Embossed wallcoverings can also be used to cover entire walls, and multi-directional patterns are suitable for ceilings. As a classy finishing touch to a room, consider using a raised border at skirting board or dado rail height, or run an embossed frieze round the room to add high level interest.

As with all wallcoverings, thorough preparation of the surfaces is essential, but embossed wallcoverings have the advantage of disguising walls or ceilings that are sound but uneven or have superficial flaws. Another advantage is that they have a long lifespan – for a quick facelift, you simply apply a fresh coat of paint.

Once the wallcovering is hung, you paint it to match your room scheme – the rich vinyl silk emulsion (satin latex) used here makes a dramatic backdrop to a dining room.

CHOOSING EMBOSSED WALLCOVERINGS

Embossed wallcoverings are sold in a range of weights and thicknesses, from light raised patterns to those that are deeply embossed. Papers with a slightly raised pattern are usually the cheapest – to avoid overstretching, take care when pasting that you don't fill the hollows with adhesive. Deep embossed wallcoverings are made from cotton fibres rather than paper, and are less likely to stretch.

Lincrusta, with a solid, linoleum-like surface, is the heaviest and most durable of embossed wallcoverings. Before you buy, make sure you want to live with Lincrusta for some time – it's difficult to remove, but you can redecorate it again and again.

Lightweight relief wallcoverings such as blown vinyls are not embossed but are made from a moulded layer of expanded vinyl bonded to a paper backing. Their insulating properties help to reduce condensation, making them ideal for covering walls in a kitchen or bathroom. They are the simplest relief wallcoverings to work with because there are no hollows on the paper backing, which makes pasting easier, or you can choose from a range of ready-pasted blown vinyls. When you redecorate, blown vinyl is much easier to strip than other relief wallcoverings.

Most embossed wallcoverings are sold in standard rolls 10m (33ft) long and 52cm (20½in) wide. Some heavy embossed coverings are available in pre-trimmed panels of various sizes to use under a dado rail or as decorative panels.

HANGING EMBOSSED WALLCOVERINGS

As with all wallcoverings, thoroughly prepare the walls before you start work – strip off old paper and ensure surfaces are smooth, clean, firm and dry. Techniques for hanging most relief coverings are the same as for all wallcoverings, except that you never use a seam roller on an embossed finish and you must butt-join and not overlap the seams. Other points to bear in mind are described below. Solid wallcoverings such as Lincrusta need special treatment – see the opposite page.

▶ Heavyweight Lincrusta dado panels topped by a stylish embossed border add Edwardian elegance to a hall. Once painted these panels are ideal for areas of heavy wear.

Crosslining the walls Before putting up an embossed wallcovering, crossline the prepared walls with lining paper – this is a good idea for all embossed wallcoverings, and is essential on gloss or solvent-based surfaces and before hanging a heavy covering such as Lincrusta. To crossline, hang the lining paper horizontally on walls and at right angles to the final direction of the wallcovering on ceilings.

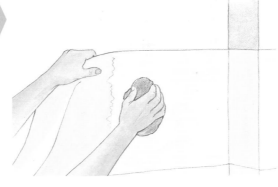

Avoiding damage Before you buy embossed wallcoverings, check the edges of the rolls and reject any that are even slightly cracked or damaged. Carry and store the rolls on their sides, to protect the edges – any damage will show at the seams, marring the finished result.

▼ Painted panels and borders add instant character to walls and help hide superficial flaws.

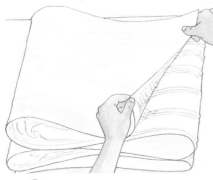

Choosing and using adhesive Use the adhesive recommended by the manufacturer – this is usually an all purpose adhesive containing a fungicide; for Lincrusta and other heavyweights, use a special glue. To avoid stretching the covering, take care not to fill the hollows on the back of some wallcoverings. Fold loosely after pasting, to avoid creasing, and follow the recommended soaking times, where appropriate, so that the wallcovering is pliable for hanging.

HANGING DADO PANELS

By far the easiest way of hanging a solid embossed wallcovering such as Lincrusta is to use pre-trimmed dado panels below a border or rail. If you have an existing dado rail, buy panel lengths to fit the wall beneath. Otherwise, finish off the top edge by hanging a Lincrusta border or adding a moulded dado rail.

> ### YOU WILL NEED
> ❖ TAPE MEASURE, PENCIL
> ❖ SPIRIT LEVEL, PLUMB LINE
> ❖ DADO PANELS
> ❖ SPONGE, soft CLOTHS
> ❖ PASTING TABLE, BRUSH
> ❖ LINCRUSTA GLUE OR VINYL-OVER-VINYL GLUE
> ❖ CRAFT KNIFE or SCISSORS

1 Measuring up If you have no dado rail, measure the length of the dado panel and use a spirit level to mark a horizontal line along the wall from which to hang the panels. Drop a plumb line to mark a vertical guideline for the first panel.

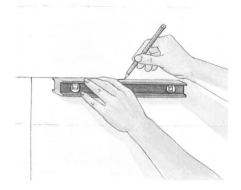

2 Soaking the backing Sponge the paper backing of each panel with warm water and leave them to soak, stacked flat back to back, for 20-30 minutes or as recommended by manufacturer. Wipe off surplus water with a dry cloth.

3 Applying glue Brush the Lincrusta or vinyl-over-vinyl glue on to the back of the first panel. If the glue is too thick to spread, stir vigorously but do not dilute. Make sure the whole surface, especially the edges, is evenly covered.

4 Hanging the panels Hang the first panel immediately you have applied the glue, aligning the top with your guideline or the dado rail and one edge with the vertical line. Smooth into position with a cloth pad, paying particular attention to edges – do not use a seam roller. Wipe off any surplus glue, and continue glueing and hanging panels.

5 Turning corners If the corner is well rounded, ease the panel round the angle, making sure the seam does not fall near an outward angle. For a sharp corner, cut and hang the panel in two sections, butting the cut edges together at the corner – do not overlap. When you are cutting the panel, use a craft knife and angle the cut slightly for a mitred finish.

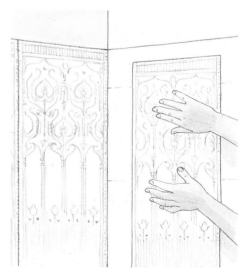

6 Finishing off Leave the panels to dry for at least a couple of days. If necessary, fill any imperfections at corners with a little putty. Allow to dry then prepare the surfaces for painting by wiping down the panels with a cloth dipped in white (mineral) spirit.

PAINTING EMBOSSED WALLCOVERINGS

Leave the wallcovering to dry out thoroughly before painting. Check through the details below to find the right type of paint for the wallcovering you are using. Either paint in the normal way, using a soft brush to work the paint well into the recesses, or try a simple paint technique to emphasize the raised pattern.

Medium/light embossed, blown vinyls Most water- or solvent/oil-based paints are suitable – depending on the finish you want, a matt or silk emulsion (flat or satin latex) or a solvent/oil-based satin or gloss paint all give a good result. Build up several coats of colour until you get the desired effect.

Heavy embossed For solid, oil-based wallcoverings like Lincrusta you must use a solvent/oil-based paint as a first coat – a water-based paint won't adhere. Use either an eggshell or a gloss finish. If you prefer a matt finish, use a solvent/oil-based paint under two or more coats of emulsion – bear in mind that this finish is not as durable as a completely solvent/oil-based system.

Special techniques Experiment with a simple paint technique to enhance the overall effect of the wallcovering. Brush on a base coat of the right type of paint for the wallcovering as described above and leave to dry. Working in sections, quickly brush on a tinted glaze, or a second colour of paint, then use a soft cloth to rub off some of the wet glaze or paint from the raised pattern to leave colour in the recesses. Leave to dry and repeat the process if you want a greater depth of colour.

▲ *Because an embossed wallcovering can be sealed with several coats of paint, it is suitable for all areas of the home, even a steamy bathroom. The rich colour on these walls is a perfect match for the blue floor tiles.*

◄ *To emphasize the emboss on this wall frieze, a tinted glaze was applied over a base coat and then wiped off the raised surfaces.*

▲ *To add character to your walls, experiment with different effects and colours on a spare piece of wallcovering. For the subtle blue finish, emulsion was lightly wiped on with a cloth, and then wiped off the emboss to reveal the white base coat. For the reddish effect, a tinted glaze was brushed over a pale base coat, and then wiped off the raised area.*

WORKING WITH WALLPAPER

*Use a wallcovering to transform a room with colour,
pattern and texture – it can also be the best solution for disguising
less than perfect walls.*

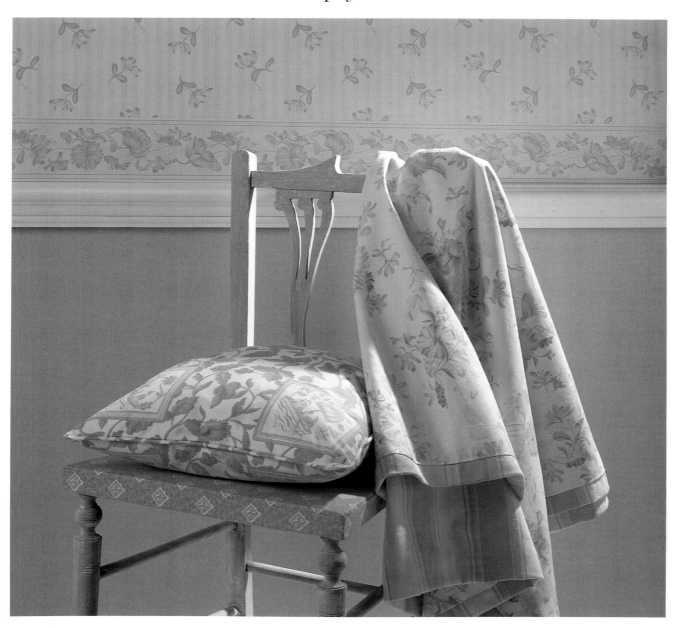

There's a huge range of wallcovering designs on the market – classics include florals, mini-prints and stripes. If you don't want to limit yourself to one design, try a combination of plain and patterned, or consider a coordinated range – many floral wallpapers are designed to team with a mini-print, with the two papers linked by colour or motif. The same pattern theme is often available in furnishing fabrics, giving lots of mix-and-match opportunities.

When choosing wallcovering, get a large sample or buy a single roll and pin some up in the room for a few days, to check the effect in both natural and artificial light. Buy all the wallpaper you need at the start, checking that the batch numbers are the same. Some stores allow you to return unopened rolls – check when you buy. An extra roll may be useful for making good any future worn areas. If you should find you've underestimated and are forced to buy more paper from a different batch, try to use the odd roll where it won't show. Always read the label on the roll before you start hanging a wallcovering as the method may vary.

A well-hung, traditional floral wallpaper, teamed with a toning plain wallpaper below the dado rail, gives a smart, decorative finish to a wall. The dado rail itself provides a guideline against which to fix a coordinating border.

HANGING WALLPAPER

YOU WILL NEED

- ❖ WALLPAPER
- ❖ PLUMB LINE
- ❖ PENCIL, METAL RULE, STEEL TAPE MEASURE
- ❖ PASTING TABLE
- ❖ Long and short-bladed SCISSORS
- ❖ WALLPAPER ADHESIVE made up as directed
- ❖ PASTING BRUSH
- ❖ STEPLADDER
- ❖ PAPERHANGING BRUSH or SPONGE
- ❖ SEAM ROLLER
- ❖ CLOTHS for mopping up

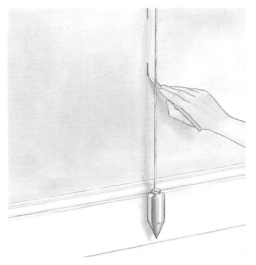

1 Marking a straight line To ensure the wallpaper hangs straight, suspend a plumbline to mark points on a vertical line against which the first drop will be hung.

2 Cutting the drop Lay wallpaper face up on the pasting table and measure out the first length adding 15cm (6in) to allow for trimming at top and bottom. Make sure that a full pattern motif will be at the top of the wall where it is most obvious. Pencil in the cutting line, check that it is straight, then cut with long-bladed scissors.

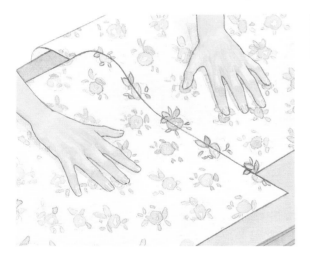

3 Matching the pattern Check the next length against the first one to match the pattern across the join. Pencil in the cutting line, then cut along it. From now on, measure up and cut all lengths as the first. Mark the top of each length to avoid hanging patterns upside-down.

4 Pasting Follow instructions on the paper for soak times. To paste paper, lay the first length face down, one side aligned with the table edge. Working quickly, paste from the centre outwards, spreading paste evenly right to the edges over half the length.

5 Folding the paper Fold the pasted paper in half, pasted sides together. Move the folded section along so it hangs over table end; paste remaining paper. Fold the second half over, leaving a gap in the middle. To carry paper to wall, drape it over your arm.

GETTING STARTED

FIXTURES AND FITTINGS
The clearer the walls the easier it is to paper them. Anything fixed to the walls with wallplugs is best removed. Push matchsticks into the wallplugs – they will stand out under the wallpaper as you hang it, to mark the position for rehanging the fittings.

PREPARING THE WALLS
The wall surfaces must be sound before you start wallpapering. Remove old wallpaper, make good any poor plaster and fill cracks. Sand down any repairs and lightly sand over all the walls before you paper.

SIZING THE WALLS
Seal new plaster with size – this is a watered down adhesive which seals the plaster and provides slip so the wallpaper slides easily into position. Leave at least an hour between sizing and papering.

THE FIRST DROP
Start alongside the largest window and plan to work away from the light, so that if any edges do overlap they will not cast a shadow and look obvious. Centre large-patterned papers on a focal point such as a chimney breast, then work outwards in both directions from that point.

TIP
HIDING THE JOIN

A wallpaper border not only adds a neat and attractive finish to your redecorated walls, it also helps disguise an untidy edge between wall and ceiling or skirting board.
There's a range of borders to suit most wallcoverings, and some manufacturers produce papers with coordinating borders. Make sure you choose an adhesive that's specially made for the border of your choice.

6 Hanging the paper Using a stepladder to reach the top of the wall, unfold the upper half of the paper leaving the lower fold still in place. Overlap the top edge on to the ceiling or cornice by 8cm (3in) with a full pattern motif at the top. Slide wallpaper into position, aligning the edge with the vertical guideline on the wall.

7 Brushing on to the wall Use a paper-hanging brush or sponge to press paper against the wall – brush down the centre, then out to the edges. If the paper bubbles or wrinkles, gently peel it off to release air and brush it back into place – little bubbles often disappear as paper dries. Unfold lower half and brush it out in the same way.

8 Trimming the edges Press the top edge into the angle between the wall and ceiling with the back of a scissor blade. Peel back the paper, cut along the crease and use the tip of the hanging brush to dab the paper back into place. Trim the lower edge in the same way. Wipe off paste from the ceiling or woodwork and pasting table with a damp cloth or sponge.

9 Matching the pattern Paste and hang the next drop, matching the pattern exactly by sliding the paper up or down using the palms of your hands. Brush into place and trim as before. Gently run a seam roller over the join about 20 minutes after hanging. Don't roll embossed papers – dab the seams firmly with the hanging brush.

SPECIAL TECHNIQUES

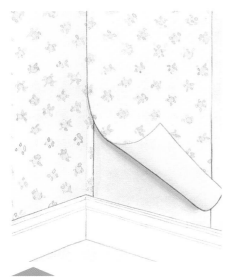

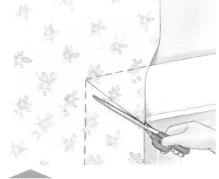

Turning a corner Hang paper that turns a corner as two strips. Measure the distance from the last drop to the corner. For internal corners, add 1.5cm (⅝in); for external corners add 3.5cm (1⅜in). Cut a length of paper to this width; hang it with the cut edge brushed into and around the corner. Measure the width of the rest of the paper then measure this distance from the corner. Hang a plumbline from this point and mark a vertical line. Hang the paper to this line, with your cut edge in the corner, overlapping the amount carried round from the adjoining wall.

Papering around doors and windows Hang the length in the normal way, but allow it to hang over the closed door. Make a diagonal cut into the corner. Trim paper roughly to the shape of the frame, allowing about 2.5cm (1in) overlap. Brush the paper into the angle between wall and frame, mark a crease line with the back of the scissors and trim.

Using lining paper Paper that is to be painted should be hung vertically as for standard wallpaper. If it is going under a wallcovering, hang it horizontally to avoid joins coinciding. Use the same paste that will be used for the final wallcovering. Start at the ceiling level and work down, butting joins closely. Leave to dry for 24 hours. Lightly sand down overlapping edges.

Papering around switches and sockets Paper straight over a switch or socket, using a sharp knife to make diagonal cuts to the corners (or several cuts if it is circular). Press the flaps back into position and trim the edges.

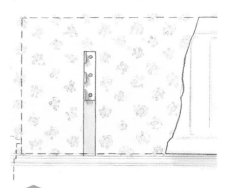

Papering around radiators Let the paper hang over the face of the radiator, and cut out a strip from the bottom of the length so that the paper can pass either side of the radiator bracket. Tuck paper behind radiator, smooth down as far as possible and trim. Check visibility of coverage along bottom, and patch from below if necessary.

Papering a window recess Paper the inside of the recess first, bringing a 5cm (2in) flap up on to the surrounding wall. Then paper the wall round the window, cutting round the shape of the window and pasting over the flap.

Once the electricity is switched off at the mains, some switches can be unscrewed from the wall and the wallpaper trimmed and tucked underneath for a really neat finish.

WALLPAPERING A CEILING

Wallpapering a ceiling provides a perfect base for painting over or, on its own, highlights a further dimension of any room. Take care to do a neat job and you won't object to anyone raising their eyes.

W hether soaking in a bubble bath, relaxing with your feet up on the sofa or just lying in bed, you'll no doubt find yourself gazing up at the ceiling. In fact, the ceiling is an area of the room that gets more attention than you might expect, and certainly has a significant effect on the way the entire room looks. For example, if you paint or paper it in a paler colour than the surrounding walls, the effect is to visually elevate the ceiling and create a more spacious feeling. In contrast, a darker ceiling gives the impression of being lower, making the room feel more cosy.

From a practical point of view, papering the ceiling lets you hide a surface that is less than perfect. The wallpaper disguises imperfections and hairline cracks so, even if you use only lining paper, you can achieve a better finish than with paint alone. Textured, embossed and woodchip papers are particularly good for hiding flaws. But don't expect them to work wonders – wallpaper won't hold together a badly cracked ceiling. If there are a lot of cracks consider using a textured paint, or maybe even fitting a new plasterboard ceiling.

For a dramatic effect in this bathroom a bold stripe wallpaper wraps around the room and continues overhead, to give a fanciful, tented feel.

PAPERING THE CEILING

When choosing wallpaper for a ceiling, remember that a small, subdued design has a more relaxing feel than a large, bold one which constantly draws the eyes upwards. In a small room, especially, a very large print might be too distracting or oppressive. Also think about the weight of the paper; a heavyweight paper is tiring to work with when you are holding it above your head. But don't go for a thin, cheap paper either, that might stretch and tear when wet.

Plan to start papering across the width of the room so you can work with shorter lengths of paper, starting at the end with fewer architectural features like alcoves and chimney breasts. If possible work away from the main light source. When the ceiling slopes, the paper looks better if the strips are running up the slope.

A standard roll of wallpaper is 10m (33ft) long by 53cm (21in) wide. Measure the width of the room, divide it by the roll width and round this figure up to the nearest whole number, to work out how many strips you need (**A**). Measure the length of the room and multiply this figure by **A** to find the length of paper you need (**B**). Divide **B** by the roll length and round up to the nearest whole number to calculate how many rolls you need. In an L-shaped room divide the room into two smaller rectangles, work out the requirements for each and add the two together.

If you don't want to do the calculation above, or you are dealing with an irregular shaped room, you can refer to the ready-reckoner chart below as a guide to the number of rolls you need. Make sure that they all come from the same batch and buy an extra roll in case of mistakes – most shops take back unopened rolls within a reasonable time span.

Distance round perimeter of room		Number of rolls
Metres	Feet	
10	33	2
11	36	2
12	39	2
13	42	3
14	46	3
15	49	4
16	52	4
17	55	4
18	58	5
19	62	5
20	65	5
21	68	6
22	72	7
23	75	7

1 Preparing the area Move furniture out of the room or away from the area you are going to start working in. Cover the furniture and floor with clean dust sheets. Construct a work platform so that you can reach the ceiling easily without stretching. Prepare the ceiling surface in the normal way; if necessary remove any existing wallcoverings and size bare plaster with dilute wallpaper adhesive.

2 Marking the first strip Measure and mark either side of the ceiling 50cm (20in) from the clearest short wall. Cut a piece of string just longer than the width of the room. Cover the string with French chalk and pin it tightly between the two marks. Pull the string slightly and then snap it to leave a chalk mark on the ceiling. Remove the string.

3 Cutting the strips Measure the width of the room. Add 10cm (4in) to this measurement to allow for trimming and pattern matching. Cut the first strip to this length. Measure and cut all the subsequent strips against the first one to match up any patterns. Mark the wrong side of the top edge of each strip so you hang all the strips in the same direction. Set aside all the lengths ready for pasting.

4 Pasting the paper Paste the paper in the usual way, remembering to brush the adhesive out from the centre right over the edges. Fold the length up concertina-wise, making each fold about 40cm (16in) wide. Drape the paper over a cardboard tube or a spare unwrapped roll of wallpaper to carry it. Climb on to the work platform.

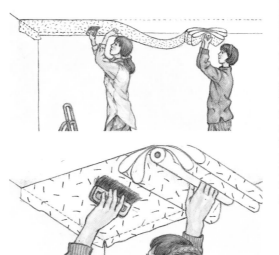

5 Positioning the first strip If you have help, ask your assistant to hold the folded paper while you position the free end; otherwise hold it yourself. Slide the top edge of the paper in place, overlapping the wall by 5cm (2in) and aligning its outside edge with the marked line. Brush the paper into place. Gradually move along the platform, unfolding the paper and brushing it out as you go.

6 Trimming the paper

Make a snip into the paper at both end corners. Run the back edge of the wallpaper scissors along the join between the wall and ceiling to crease the paper. Carefully peel the paper back. If you are papering the walls as well, trim the paper 1cm (⅜in) below the crease line. If you are just papering the ceiling, cut along the crease line. Brush the paper back into place.

By drawing your attention upwards, a ceiling paper enhances features such as this decorative cornicing. For a perfect finish, take care to neatly trim the paper to the edge of the moulding.

7 Hanging subsequent strips

Continue papering along the room, matching the pattern and butting the edges together. Use a seam roller to smooth the joins, or a wallpapering brush if you are using embossed paper. Trim each strip at the ends.

8 Hanging the last strip

Measure the space left for the last strip. If it is less than 50cm (20in) wide, add 2.5cm (1in) to the width measurement and then mark and cut the last strip to this size. Hang the paper, butting it up to the previous strip and then trim the end and side edges as in step 6.

SPECIAL TECHNIQUES

Papering around a chimney breast If there is an obstacle, such as a chimney breast, hang the wallpaper up to the obstacle and then roughly trim the paper to shape with a sharp trimming knife. Make a release cut at the corner and brush into place. Use the back edge of a pair of scissors to crease the edges of the paper around the obstacle. Then carefully trim along the crease marks.

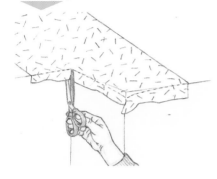

In an attic room with sloping ceilings try to hang the wallpaper in one length over walls and ceiling to avoid obvious joins. Then use separate strips where the ceiling flattens out.

Papering around a centrepiece Try to position the lengths of wallpaper so that the ceiling centrepiece lies between two strips of paper. Hang the strips up to the centrepiece and then trim the paper to fit roughly around the centrepiece. Make further radial cuts as necessary to fit exactly around the centrepiece. Use a sharp trimming knife to trim carefully all round the edge of the centrepiece.

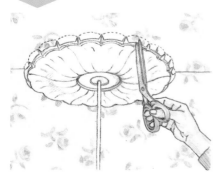

PAPERING ROUND A LIGHT FITTING

1 Hanging the paper Before hanging the strip that covers the light fitting, turn off the electricity at the mains. Remove the light bulb and shade. Hang the paper up to the light fitting. Hold the paper over the fitting and mark the position of the flex. Cut a cross at the mark, and slip the lampholder and flex through it. Hang the remaining lengths of the wallpaper.

2 Trimming the paper Make radial cuts from the small cut outwards, just wide enough to fit the light fitting cover through. Unscrew the cover and slip it through the paper. Use the tips of the papering brush to force the paper into place around the fitting and then trim it using a sharp trimming knife. Screw the cover back in place, then replace the shade and light bulb and restore the electricity supply.

Removing wallcoverings

If your walls are decorated with any finish other than paint, you must usually strip them back to bare plaster before redecorating.

Some wall and ceiling finishes – embossed wallcoverings, woodchip papers and brush-on textured materials – are intended to be overpainted when you want a change of colour scheme. But all of these, and any printed wallcoverings, must be removed completely if you want to hang a new wallcovering. How you go about this depends on what you're trying to remove but it's nearly always a messy business, so clear the surrounding area and cover the floor before you start, and have a good supply of refuse sacks for all the debris.

You don't need much equipment for removing most wallcoverings. The traditional method is to soak the walls with warm water to loosen the paper – use a wide stripping knife, and a perforating tool for scoring washable wallcoverings. For really fast stripping, or to remove certain types of wallcoverings, either hire or buy a steam stripper. The chart below tells you how to deal with different types of wallcoverings; the main methods are described overleaf.

What's on the wall already?

If you're not sure what type of wallcovering has been hung, hold a wet sponge against the wall. If it soaks up water, it is an ordinary *printed wallpaper*. If it doesn't soak up water, try to lift a corner at skirting board level to see if the coated surface layer will separate from the backing paper. If it will, it's a *vinyl wallcovering*; if not, it's a *washable wallpaper*.

How to strip wallcoverings

Wallcovering	Stripping method
Uncoated – plain and non-washable printed paper	Soak or use a steam stripper and scrape. Ready pasted types peel off easily if they are left to soak; others may need scraping as well, depending on the thickness.
Coated – washable paper coated with a thin film of PVC	Score the surface of the wallpaper first then soak or steam strip and scrape; allow plenty of time for the water to penetrate the outer resistant coating.
Vinyl – plastic washable coating with a thin film of PVC	First carefully peel off the outer vinyl layer from the paper backing in whole lengths. Strip the paper backing by soaking or steaming and then scraping.
Plain lining paper – usually emulsion painted, but may be found under surface paper	Score the surface then soak or steam and strip. Water must be given time to penetrate behind the paint. Determined scraping is necessary if the paint has soaked into the paper.
Woodchip – textured lining paper in which wood pulp is sandwiched	Score and steam strip. Try to prevent layers separating and avoid prolonged steaming on plasterboard or if the plaster is in poor condition.
Embossed – relief wallcoverings containing plaster and other additives or with an expanded vinyl pattern. May be printed or painted	Score first before steam stripping. The task will be easier if you let the steam soften the paint coating thoroughly before attempting to scrape.
Fabric – speciality wallcoverings such as hessian and grasscloth which are usually hung with heavy duty adhesive	Dry-strip by lifting a corner and pulling the length upwards, as when stripping vinyls. Alternatively, use a steam wallpaper stripper first to soften the adhesive.
Textured finishes – removing a textured finish is time-consuming; it may be quicker to skim a fresh coat of plaster over the finish	Soften and strip with a steam stripper. If the steam stripper doesn't loosen it, the finish is probably a modern texture paint, which can only be stripped with a special texture paint remover.

Stripping walls

Printed wallpaper or unpainted lining paper can usually be removed quite simply by soaking the surface with plenty of water and then scraping off the softened paper. For fast stripping, or to deal with wallcoverings which have been painted over or are tricky to remove, a steam wallpaper stripping machine is much more effective. Whichever system you use, first inspect the wallcovering to see if any special treatment is necessary before you begin the stripping operation.

Scoring the surface Before you start stripping, speed up penetration of the water or steam by scoring the top layer with a perforating tool – scoring is very important on painted and washable wallcoverings. Apply just enough pressure to score the wallcovering, not the wall.

Peeling off vinyl For easy stripping, the top layer of a vinyl wallcovering is designed to peel away from the backing paper. Lift a corner of the vinyl; pulling upwards, peel the entire length off the wall. Remove the backing by stripping by hand or machine.

Soaking and stripping

1 Soaking Use a spray bottle to soak the walls – it is less messy than sponges or cloths. Spray an area of about 1 sq m (10 sq ft) at a time, allowing the water to soak in for a few minutes.

2 Stripping Scrape off the wet paper with a wide stripping knife – it has a stiffer blade than a filling knife, which would dig into the wall surface.

3 Cleaning Wash down the walls to remove any remaining paper. Stubborn areas may need repeated spraying and scraping.

Using a steam stripper

A steam stripper is a simple tool that removes wallcoverings very effectively. A heated water tank supplies steam to a flat plate which is pressed against the wallcovering – when the adhesive is softened the wallcovering can usually be scraped off quite easily. Some domestic strippers are rather like a steam iron – you hold the all-in-one machine to the wall. Others have a separate steam plate attached by a hose to a larger capacity water tank.

Take care when using a steam stripper – steam can scald or, used incorrectly, the machine can damage walls or other surfaces. Too much steam can damage plasterboard walls. Watch the amount of time you hold the plate against the surface: use the minimum amount of steam required to loosen the paper. Test a small area before you tackle an entire wall. In hard water areas, fill the tank with distilled or demineralized water. To stop steam loosening lining paper on the ceiling, tape plastic sheeting over the area of ceiling above where you are working.

1 Building up steam Protect the area around which you will be working – you need to plan to work up the wall so that the rising steam starts to soften the wallcovering above. Fill the tank with water, following the instructions. Plug in at the mains socket, switch on and wait until a good head of steam builds up.

2 Loosening the paper Holding the machine in your less favoured hand and a wide stripping knife in the other, press the stripper directly on to the wall for 10-20 seconds, depending on the type of paper – keep checking to see if the wallcovering has loosened.

3 Stripping Scrape off the loosened wallcovering, directing the stripper at the next section of wall as you work. With a little practice you can build up a rhythm of work, so you steam and scrape adjacent areas simultaneously, but never apply the stripper to one place for longer than necessary.

4 Finishing off After stripping the wallcovering, wash the walls down to remove any traces of paste and paper.

SAFE STEAM STRIPPING

❖ Use according to instructions.
❖ Wear thick gloves and cover your arms to guard against scalding; wear goggles to protect your eyes against sudden spurts of steam.
❖ Don't touch the base of the steamer during or just after use, and take care where you point the steam outlet.
❖ Between use always lay the stripper down with the steam outlet side up.
❖ Keep the outlet holes clear of debris.
❖ Unplug the machine at the mains before refilling and when it's not in use.
❖ Empty the tank and allow to cool before storing.
❖ Take care not to over reach, and work at a comfortable height, particularly when working from a ladder.

WALLPAPER PANELLING

Give your room a graceful eighteenth century air with elegant mock panelling cleverly created from lengths of wallcovering and framed with wallpaper border.

Wallpaper panels are a wonderful way of adding decoration to painted walls, and if you haven't wallpapered before, this is a perfect introduction. You just cut your chosen wallcovering into lengths , hang it as panels round the wall and then use a wallpaper border to frame each panel.

Try positioning a panel each side of a fireplace or hang them inside an alcove. Or use three panels to break up a large, featureless expanse of wall. Wallpaper panels also look good positioned above a dado rail, with the walls painted in different plain colours above and below.

You can make your panels from any patterned wallpaper. The panel design can be one single large pattern repeat, several smaller repeats or an all-over pattern such as a stripe. As you only need fairly small amounts to create a spectacular effect, you can go for more expensive wallpaper designs if these take your fancy.

Wallpaper borders can coordinate with the panel or you could create the impression of architectural moulding with a classical design such as a simple beading or rope effect or perhaps a traditional pattern. There's no need to hang lining paper under the panel – you can hang the panels straight on to plain painted walls.

Hang classical style wallpaper panels for a sophisticated look. Here, a single pattern repeat is exactly the right size for a panel.

HANGING WALLPAPER PANELS

Decide how many panels you want around the room and the space to be left between them. Wallpaper rolls are usually 10m (33ft) long and 53cm (21in) wide – if possible make the panels the same width as the wallpaper so that there's no need to

trim the edges. If the existing painted walls are in good condition, all that needs to be done is to wash them down and then leave them to dry before hanging the panels. Select the adhesive appropriate for the wallcovering you want to use.

1 Positioning the panels Work out roughly what size each panel needs to be. Find the centre of the wall and work out the position of all the panels.

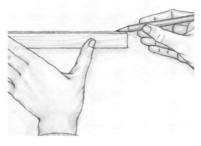

2 Marking the wall Using a spirit level and metal straightedge, lightly pencil in two horizontal lines to mark the position of the top and bottom of the panels on the wall. Remember that the border adds to both the height and depth of the panel. If desired, also mark in side verticals using a plumb line.

3 Drawing out panels Unroll the wallpaper. Measure and mark off the correct lengths. Using a straightedge and set square, draw straight lines along the top and bottom of each panel. Make sure that all the designs match up before cutting out.

4 Cutting out the panels Cut along pencil lines using a craft knife and straightedge. Unroll border and cut strips two border's width longer than panel edges.

5 Hanging the panels For paper that must be pasted, apply adhesive as recommended by the manufacturer, going right up to the edges. Soak pre-pasted paper as instructed. Hang the paper panel from the top pencil line. Smooth the paper from the centre outwards, working down the panel with a wallpaper brush or sponge.

◤ *A richly patterned floral wallpaper could look overpowering covering an entire wall. It is more pleasing to the eye when used as stylish panels.*

FRAMING THE PANEL

When choosing your border, remember you need to mitre it at the corners. Simple patterns are the easiest to match; you may have to adjust more complicated patterns slightly to avoid unsightly joins.

1 Sticking the border Paste or soak the border strips and butt join around the edges of the panel. Overlap the ends at each corner, adjusting the borders for a neat mitre if necessary.

2 Mitring the corners Using a ruler and a craft knife, cut across the diagonal through both overlapped layers to make a neat mitre. Remove the trimmings, stick down the corners and press the whole border with a seam roller.

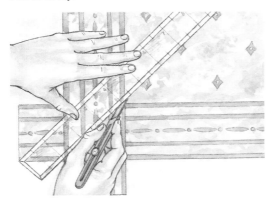

▶ *Bordered wallpaper panels are a stylish and original way of making use of the coordinated ranges available.*

▼ *Wallpaper panels can be hung over papered walls too. You can use contrasting patterns as long as the colours are complementary.*

WALLPAPER BORDERS

Take a new line on wallpaper borders and use them in imaginative ways to add character to your home – a border is one of the easiest, and least expensive, ways of adding a near-instant lift to a room.

F raming a window, surrounding a mirror or forming a decorative panel – there's an infinite number of ways that wallpaper borders can be put to work to make a room special. If you are planning to add a border at dado or ceiling height around a room, look at the obstacles in the way; it may be more effective to take the border up around a fireplace or doorway than stop it on either side.

Or dispense altogether with the idea of using the border in a traditional way. Create mock panels along a wall with a favourite border and paper the centre with a coordinating design – it's an economical way of using expensive papers.

Furniture and accessories, too, can be given a lift with an unexpected use of borders. Line the shelves of a dresser with a border to complement your china, cover hat boxes for a pretty storage idea, or cut out the motifs from border scraps to decorate stationery, waste paper bins, lampshades or storage jars so they match the rest of the room.

Lighten the recesses of open shelving with wallpaper and a matching border, picked to flatter the china display.

▶ Frame panels of a favourite wallpaper with a coordinating border to give a plain wall instant impact. New on the market are corner motifs, which eliminate the need for tricky mitring of corners.

▼ The deep border with its lively street scene picks up all the colours of the room and provides plenty of visual entertainment at bedtime. There's a wide range of borders for children's bedrooms on the market – some have an alphabetical or number theme, and are educational as well as fun.

▲ Define the graceful proportions of a fireplace with a border. This delicate floral border introduces welcome pattern into a plain room and forms a clever link with the dainty china plates on the wall.

◀ Inexpensive bathroom fittings come up trumps with the imaginative use of a border. The border fulfils the traditional role of a dado, then trims plain cupboard doors and gives a small mirror prominence.

DECORATIVE BORDERS

*Whether you want to pep up existing wall finishes
or add style to a new scheme, there's a wallpaper border to suit
every room in the house.*

There's an enticing range of borders available, in widths that range from a narrow 5cm (2in) strip to wide 18cm (7in) bands, so it's easy to find one to suit every room. Patterns include simple bands of colour, geometric designs and floral patterns. You can also get relief borders with raised patterns that look like traditional plaster mouldings.

Borders are simple to hang and can be added to any sound, untextured surface. For a new scheme, look at coordinated ranges of wallcover-ings and borders. If your wallcovering or paint is in good condition but the room needs a quick lift, stick a border over the existing finishes. With some borders, you don't even need paste – just peel off the backing strip and stick them in place.

As well as providing an elegant finishing touch, a border at picture or dado rail height adds character to a featureless room or gives an impression of pleasing proportions. Use a border to emphasize good points, too, by running one round a handsome fireplace, window or alcove.

Teamed with matching paint on woodwork, this delicate shell border runs above a dado rail and is carried round to frame a door.

POSITIONING A BORDER

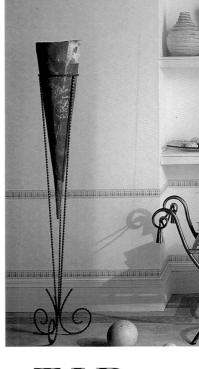

A well placed border in a room can do wonders to highlight strengths and help disguise weaknesses. A border at picture rail height makes the ceiling appear lower, while placing one around a window frame or fireplace draws the eye to the feature, making it seem larger. If you're lucky enough to have traditional architectural features such as dado rails and covings, run a border beside them to make them the focus of attention. If you haven't dado rails or covings, use borders as eye-catching substitutes.

The easiest way to use a border is to run it horizontally, parallel to the floor. A horizontal border is usually at ceiling, picture rail, dado rail or skirting board level.

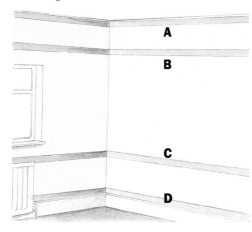

A Ceiling level A border at the top of the wall creates a neat finish, and adds interest if you haven't a coving or cornice.

B Picture rail level To make a ceiling appear lower or to break up an expanse of wall, place a border above or below the picture rail or, if you haven't a rail, about 30-45cm (12-18in) down.

C Dado rail level Dado rails are usually just under a third of the way between floor and ceiling. Use a border at this height to separate two different wallcoverings – perhaps an expensive paper above a painted embossed wallcovering.

D Skirting board level A border makes a neat finish to the foot of a wall, and enhances a plain skirting board. To add interest to a high stairwell, run a border above the skirting up the stairs, with a matching border at ceiling height.

GETTING STARTED

How much to buy Most borders are sold in standard length rolls of 10 metres (33ft). Work out how many rolls you need to run a border around a room by measuring the length and width of the room, adding the two together and multiplying by two. Add to the total the length of any additional border you want to use, for example round a door or window. Divide the total by the length of the roll, rounding up the figure to the nearest whole roll.

Hanging a border is easiest when you are laying it against an existing straight line, such as the ceiling, picture rail or skirting board. To add a border in place of a picture or dado rail, first make a horizontal guideline to make sure the border is hung straight.

Using a level Mark the position of the bottom edge of the border. Place a (spirit) level at this height and make a horizontal pencil line at each end. Repeat along the length of the border position, then join up the horizontal lines with a long steel rule or wooden batten.

Measuring height If you don't have a spirit level, measure and mark at intervals the distance from the floor or ceiling on the wall, then join up the marks with a straight edge. For a border running up a stairway, chalk a plumbline to the correct height, mark the wall at intervals and join up the marks.

To position a vertical border use the feature you are framing as a guideline – it may not be perfectly vertical but the border will look straight. For a border hung some way out from a straight edge such as a door or window, use a plumbline to mark a vertical guideline.

PREPARING SURFACES

In a room that's just been redecorated, leave fresh paint or newly hung wallcovering for at least 48 hours before hanging the border.

To add a border to an existing scheme, check that surfaces are sound. Make sure painted surfaces are smooth, clean and dry. Scrape back flaking paint to a sound edge and rub down with fine sandpaper then fill any cracks and repaint.

Wipe over or dust down wallcoverings and check they are firmly stuck down – carefully peel back any unstuck edges, paste down with special repair adhesive and leave to dry. Where the border is to go along the edge of the paper, lightly sand uneven edges.

T I P
CHECKING IT OUT
If you're not sure how a border will look, unroll a length and fix it temporarily in place with Blu-tack or a glue stick, then stand back and check the effect from different parts of the room.

▼ *This border is on a clear, self-adhesive strip – it is easy to apply and the final effect looks like a stencil.*

HANGING A BORDER

The easiest borders to hang are self-adhesive – you simply peel off a backing strip and press the border on to the wall. These are best used over painted or vinyl surfaces – if you make a mistake, you can peel them off for up to 10 minutes after sticking without damage. When fixing a self-adhesive border to wallpaper, make sure you position it accurately as it's difficult to remove the border without tearing the wallpaper. Use a special border adhesive, available from DIY stores, for a border that needs to be pasted.

SELF-ADHESIVE BORDERS

1 Positioning Unpeel about 10cm (4in) of the backing and stick the end in place, aligning one edge with the marked guideline or feature you are following.

2 Sticking down Smooth the border down with a sponge, taking care not to stretch the strip as you work. Continue along the strip, peeling and sticking and close butting joins.

PASTED BORDERS

◗ *Borders at different levels – here, at picture rail, dado rail and skirting board height – are a quick and inexpensive way of adding elegance to a plain expanse of wall.*

◗ *Many manufacturers produce matching or coordinating ranges of borders and fabrics: this alphabet design gives a child's bedroom real designer style.*

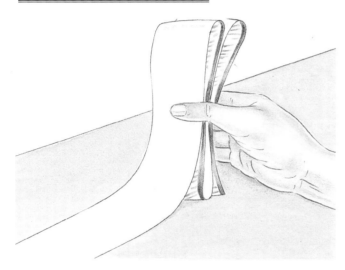

1 Applying paste Cut the border to length, then lay it face down on the pasting table. Paste down the centre, spreading it out thinly and evenly towards the edges.

2 Folding up With pasted sides together, fold up the border concertina-fashion into convenient folds of about 30cm (12in), so that you can hold it in one hand.

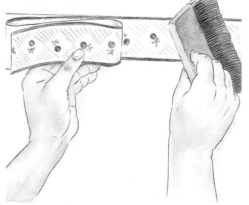

3 Sticking down If you are right-handed, hold the concertina of paper in your left hand and work from right to left – this leaves your right hand free to work. Having checked that it's the right way up, unfold about 30cm (12in) of border, align it with the guideline and press lightly into place. Smooth down with a wallpaper brush.

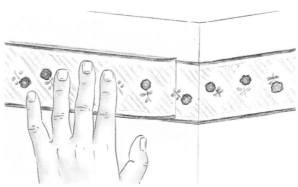

4 Rounding a corner Take the first length just around the corner. Overlap the second length slightly so the pattern matches. Lay a straight edge over overlapping pieces of paper. Cut through both pieces with a craft knife. Peel away the waste and brush down to form a perfect butt joint.

CUTTING A MITRE

The best way of dealing with angles when you are using a border to frame a door or window is to mitre the adjoining strips.

With practice the mitring technique isn't difficult and works for all angles – as well as using it for right angles round a door or window you can adapt it for awkward areas such as a sloping attic wall or a stairwell.

A mitred join with a good pattern match gives a neat, professional finish to angles when you are framing a door, window or other feature in a room.

1 Positioning Cut and paste the vertical strip, leaving an unpasted overlap of 15cm (6in) more than the border width. Cut the horizontal strip, allowing a similar overlap at either end. Blu-tack or glue stick the unpasted horizontal strip in place over the vertical strip with the pattern roughly matching at corners.

2 Marking the mitre Make light pencil marks at inner and outer points on the vertical strip where the two strips intersect. On the horizontal strip, draw a line between these two marks. On the vertical section, cut along a line drawn between the marks and paste down the strip.

3 Adjusting pattern Lightly fold the horizontal strip back along the pencil line and place it against the vertical strip. Take time to check the fit and the pattern match, adjusting the fold if necessary but keeping the angle. When you are satisfied, make a sharp crease. If working round a door or window, hang both vertical strips first, then mark mitre angles and check the fit and pattern match at both corners before marking the horizontal piece with creases.

4 Cutting the cross strip Using sharp scissors, cut along the fold line on the horizontal section. Repeat with opposite end if necessary.

5 Finishing off Paste and stick down the horizontal section, butting up to the corners of the vertical strip. Smooth firmly in place with a sponge and wipe away excess paste. Lightly firm the join with a seam roller.

DISGUISING CORNERS

A little sleight of hand is a good way of dealing with corners if the border has a pronounced motif. You can disguise the corner and keep the motif intact by cutting around the edge of the motif on either the vertical or horizontal strip. Then paste the motif so that it overlaps the other strip.

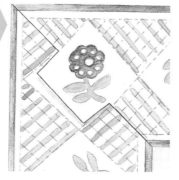

Print Rooms

Add a touch of eighteenth-century elegance to your walls with prints, borders, swags and garlands. It's easy to do, especially as photocopies of old engravings and prints look just as effective as the real thing.

Print rooms became popular in the eighteenth century when black and white engravings were inexpensive and plentiful. The prints were pasted directly on to the walls, then framed with ornamental paper borders, and linked together with loops of cord, floral swags and bows cut out of paper. The general effect was one of an elegant, if slightly crowded, trompe l'oeil picture gallery.

You don't have to cover an entire room with prints to get the same decorative effect. A display of prints can look just as charming in an alcove, along the walls of a narrow hallway, as a decorative surround for a dresser or arranged above a chest of drawers or an occasional table.

Part of the pleasure lies in collecting the material and deciding how to arrange it. You may want to stick to a single theme that you find appealing, or you may prefer to collect together a wide range of subject matter in a similar style. Instead of engravings, you can use good-quality photocopies of old prints and borders provided this does not infringe any copyright. You can also use pictures from magazines, cards, calendars and gift wrap papers, framing them with conventional wallpaper borders.

It's traditional to stick the prints on to a straw-coloured background, but any plain colour that provides a pleasing contrasting background to the black and white prints works just as well.

Bold black and white botanical prints show up beautifully against a sunny yellow background. Varying the size and shape of the prints adds visual interest to this formal arrangement.

TRADITIONAL PRINT WALLS

It is worth spending some time pre-planning your print wall. The arrangement is crucial – too few prints looks meagre but too many is overpowering.Cut out all the components and position them on the wall temporarily with Blu-tack or a glue stick. Stand well back to get a good view of the overall effect. Move the pieces around until you are happy with the result.

Many of the rules of picture grouping apply to a successfully arranged print wall. Position your most attractive prints at eye level. Aim for a pleasing, well balanced overall effect with no single print dominating the rest. To emphasize the symmetry of the layout, it is essential to keep all the prints absolutely straight and level.

Choose a variety of shapes and sizes so you can group the prints in different ways. In addition to regular square and rectangular prints, circular and oval ones add to the visual diversity. Similarly, use a good selection of paper bows, cords, tassels, chains and ribbons, interspersed with garlands and swags, to link the whole arrangement. Make sure that the decorative borders round the prints and any linking devices do not overwhelm the prints.

1 Cutting out the pieces Cut out the prints and border strips on a board, using a craft knife against a steel rule. Leave a narrow margin around each print to carry the borders. Cut the border strips to size leaving a border's width at each end for overlapping at the corners. Use nail scissors to cut out curved linkage pieces and intricate shapes.

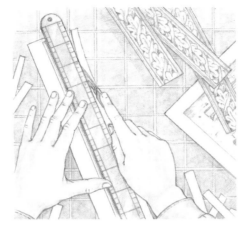

2 Planning the arrangement In a dry run, stick all the pieces on to the wall with Blu-tack and move them around until you are happy with the arrangement.

☑ *Note how the dogs on the fringes of this canine-theme display all look towards the central prints, drawing the eye into the composition.*

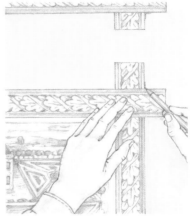

3 Marking up Check the pieces are level and evenly spaced with a tape measure and spirit level. Mark the positions of the corners of the prints and of any linking pieces lightly on the wall. Peel them off and remove Blu-tack or traces of glue.

4 Pasting up Apply a thin coat of paste to the back of one print and leave it to soak in for 30 seconds. Apply another coat and position the print on the wall. Repeat for the other prints.

△ *Classical prints create a handsome display in a formal dining room. Hand-painted, trompe l'oeil tasselled cords link the prints and add a witty detail.*

5 Smoothing out the prints
Using a dry decorating brush, gently brush from the centre of each print out towards the edges to remove any air bubbles. Press down the edges with a roller, if necessary. Don't worry if some prints bubble at this stage as they will dry flat.

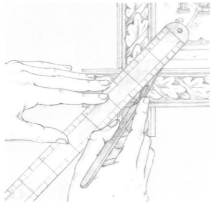

6 Pasting and mitring the borders Work on the borders of one print at a time. Paste the strips in position around the print. To mitre each corner, place a steel rule diagonally between the inside and outside corner of the border. Cut along the diagonal with a craft knife, and gently peel off the two bits of excess border.

7 Finishing touches Paste up the linking pieces in the same way as the prints and borders. When the adhesive is dry, protect the arrangement with a coat of matt varnish or acrylic sealer over the entire wall.

MODERN PRINT ROOMS

If the formal look of an eighteenth-century print room is not to your taste, dispense with tradition and try out some modern variations. Here are just a few ideas:

❖ Books devoted to out-of-copyright designs and motifs can provide a wealth of suitable material to create a print room on any theme and in any style. Photocopy interesting details from these books and space them over a wall so that they look like repeat motifs in a wallpaper.

❖ Experiment with colour. Try black and white prints framed with brightly coloured paper borders, or photocopy black and white images on coloured paper and arrange them against a white wall. You can also tint the prints with a wash of coloured ink or watercolour paint.

❖ Instead of basing your display on eighteenth and nineteenth-century engravings, make an arrangement of modern prints, book illustrations, cartoons and photographs.

▶ *Use old black and white or sepia family photographs instead of prints to build up a display with a personal feel. Two of the pictures are framed with paper borders, while others have regular, three-dimensional frames. A cloudy blue paint-effect background adds a modern touch and sets off the pictures perfectly.*

◀ *Story book illustrations of favourite nursery characters are a wonderful starting point for a gallery of prints in a child's room. To copy this charming variation on a theme, reduce or enlarge the drawings on a photocopier, and colour in the details with a wash of coloured ink or watercolour paint.*

Hanging pictures

Ensure that a picture looks its best by hanging it securely and in exactly the right place.

When hanging pictures, practical considerations are as important as artistic ones, for the picture's sake and to achieve the look you want. Although you can hang a picture on your own, you'll find it much easier with a helper. Before you begin, you need to choose the right fixings for the job.

Fixings for walls

Moulding hooks (1) These S-shaped hooks fit on to *picture rails* (2). The picture is suspended by chain or wire from the hook.

Picture hooks Shaped brass hooks are fixed to solid plaster and wooden walls with steel pins. The pins enter the wall at an angle dictated by the design of the hook for maximum strength and security. The hooks come in several sizes for different picture weights, with *single pins* (3) for lightweight pictures, or *double pins* (4) for heavier ones. They are not suitable for ceramic tiles or concrete. *Decorative picture hooks* (5) incorporating small motifs are designed to be visible when fixed in position.

Screws (6) For heavier pictures and for fixing into very hard surfaces, you can use screws or pairs of *L-hooks* (13) set into wallplugs. For ceramic tiled walls, drill a hole through the tile with a ceramic bit, and sink a wallplug well into the wall behind the tile.

Other attachments For partition walls faced with plasterboard, use *hollow wall fixings* (7) and screws. *Hooked plastic discs* (8) with strong steel pins are easy to hammer into hard plaster walls. They are available in several sizes for different picture weights.

Fixings for backs of pictures

D-rings (9) Ideal for lightweight pictures, these D-shaped rings are attached to small metal plates, which are screwed sideways into the back of the frame one-third of the way down. Cord or wire is threaded through the rings.

Glass or mirror plates (10) are screwed into the frame of heavy pictures, and keep paintings flat against the wall.

S-hooks are S-shaped rings used to attach picture chain to D-rings.

Screw eyes (11) are screws with a loop at the top and are screwed into the back of the frame to hold wire or cord – special *picture rings* (12) are available to connect the wire or cord to the screw eyes. Screw eyes are good for frames thicker than 15mm (⅝in) and can also be hooked on to L-hooks.

L-hooks (13) are screwed into the wall to correspond with screw eyes or D-rings on the frame. They make it easier to judge the hanging height and get the picture level.

Wires and cords

Brass picture wire (14) is the traditional material for hanging light and mediumweight pictures.

Nylon picture cord (15) Nowadays, cord is widely used in preference to wire. 'Invisible' nylon wire is good for lighter pictures, and inconspicuous enough to be used to hang pictures one above the other.

Picture chain (16) is used for larger paintings, attached to D-rings on the backs of pictures with S-hooks, and often hooked on to brass picture rails.

Ribbon (17) is an attractive way of hanging a row of small pictures. It can also be purely decorative, tied into a bow and attached to the top of the frame to give the impression that the picture is hanging from the ribbon. *Ready-made picture bows*, made from *ribbon* (18) or *gilded wood* (19), are available from decorating and soft furnishings shops.

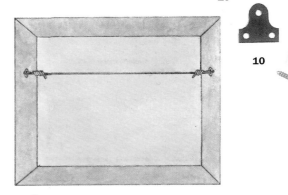

Attaching picture wire Measure the distance between the D-rings or screw eyes on the frame and cut wire 4-6cm (1½-2¼in) longer than this. Thread it through the D-rings or screw eyes and twist each end of the wire back on itself.

Positioning a picture

Getting a single picture to hang straight is fairly easy when you use picture wire or cord – once the picture is hanging on the hook you only need to slide the picture to the left or right slightly until the top is level. The real knack is to get the picture hanging exactly where you want it. Follow the steps for perfect results and remember to:

❖ Hang pictures away from direct sunlight or strong artificial light and try not to subject them to heat from radiators, fireplaces, hot water pipes or internal flues.

❖ Position pictures hung above seating higher than pushed-back chairs or backs of heads.

❖ Rest the base of heavy pictures on a table or sideboard, or attach small wood blocks to the wall to support the frame, if necessary.

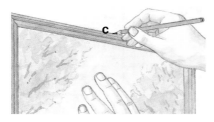

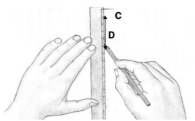

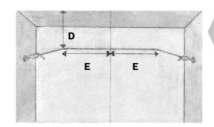

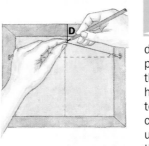

1 Establishing the position Hold the wire-hung picture in place against the wall and make a pencil mark (**C**) on the wall to show the central point of the top of the picture. Then lay the picture face-down on a table.

2 Working out the drop Draw a central line down the back of the picture. Then pull the centre of the hanging wire towards the top centre of the picture until it is taut. Mark the top point of the taut wire. Measure the distance (**D**) from the top centre of the picture down to the mark.

3 Positioning the hook Measure and mark **D** from the pencil mark on the wall (**C**) downwards, to find out where the point of the taut wire will sit. Drive a hook into the wall, so the bottom of the hook rests on this new mark.

Hanging up a picture with two hooks

If a picture is hanging in a spot where it's likely to be brushed against – a busy hallway, for example – it's safer to hang the picture with two hooks, making it more stable. Establish the position of the picture on the wall and mark the central line down the back of the picture, as described in steps 1 and 2 above.

Using two hooks Measure equal distances along the wire from the D-rings and push it upwards to establish two hanging points. Measure sideways from the central line to the hanging points (**E**), and down from the top (**D**). Mark these measurements on the wall to establish the positions of the hooks.

Fixing heavy pictures

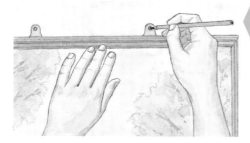

Attaching glass plates Screw the glass plates to the picture frame. Hold the picture in place on the wall, checking with a spirit level that it is straight. Pencil through the glass plate holes to mark the position of the screw holes on the wall.

Positioning L-hooks Establish the position of the picture on the wall, following step 1 above. Draw a central line down the back of the picture, then mark a line across the back from one screw eye or D-ring to the other. Measure the distance from the central line to the screw eyes or D-rings, as well as down from the top of the picture, to determine the position of the L-hooks on the wall. Lightly mark these measurements on the wall with a pencil, and fix the L-hooks in place, using wallplugs if necessary.

GENERAL CARE OF PICTURES

If a picture on paper becomes damp, remove it from its frame and place it between several sheets of thick blotting paper. Cover completely with a flat board, evenly weighted on top. Replace the blotting paper with fresh sheets frequently until all the moisture is absorbed.

❖

To clean glass, spray window cleaner on to a soft, clean cloth to prevent seepage under the frame, or use neat methylated spirit (denatured alcohol) and rub lightly.

❖

To clean plain frames, dust with a clean, soft cloth or wipe with a slightly damp cloth. For elaborate gilt frames, dust with a soft, dry paint brush.

❖

Protecting from damp walls

Use a dab of adhesive to stick a thick cork to the corners at the back of the frame, to let air circulate between the painting and the wall, preventing damage from condensation.

Picture rails

Picture rails are especially suitable for hanging large, heavy pictures in rooms with high ceilings. Old-fashioned, wooden moulding picture rails are an integral part of the architectural detailing of a house. Pictures hung from rails on special moulding hooks are quickly and easily repositioned. Their height is simply adjusted by altering the length of the picture wire, cord or chain.

GROUPING PICTURES

*Hanging pictures en masse can be as creative as the choice
of the images themselves and the overall impact much more than
the sum of the separate parts.*

Whether loosely or tightly clustered, and formally or informally arranged, pictures displayed in groups are bound to make a handsome feature. Individual small prints, paintings and photographs, which might look lost on a large expanse of wall, benefit especially from grouping. And unlike a single large picture, which is static and unchanging, you can rearrange, add to, subtract from or replace individual components of a group display as mood and budget allow, to enliven your decor and keep boredom at bay.

The group could be composed from a random collection of images you happen to like, or be limited to a single theme – subject matter such as landscapes, seascapes, portraits, flowers or cats; a colour or colour range such as black and white or soft pastels; or even a style of art, such as Oriental, abstract or Classical. Whether matching or contrasting, dominant or subtle, colours should blend with the decor.

You can use virtually invisible glass covers without any surrounds at all, or frames that range from plain, neutral strips of wood or metal to more decorative and stylized types, with pulling power of their own. Mounts, too, can be pale or boldly colourful. Using identical frames and mounts reinforces the sense of unity, particularly if they are in keeping with the decor – heavy and ornate in an opulent decor, natural wood in a country-cottage style. On the other hand, a cheerful medley of mix and match frames and mounts reflects an informal, relaxed approach to interior design.

A double row of historical portrait miniatures acts as a frame for a large central portrait. Flanking mirrors reflect another portrait on the opposite wall, and the soft yellow roses and fragrant stocks emphasize the feminine imagery.

▲ *A sense of ordered liveliness* comes from hanging slightly different sized square and rectangular frames close together, with the space between the frames forming an attractive pattern in its own right.

▾ *Victorian botanical prints*, coloured by hand, have an individual charm and delicacy. Here, prints of tender succulents in identical mounts and frames combine the formality and floral theme of the room.

▲ *Concentrating on the Classical*, this symmetrical display of rectangular prints of busts and urns, interspersed with cameos in oval frames, suits the subject matter and subdues the boisterous decor at the same time.

IN THE FRAME

Rather than hang any old pictures just for the sake of having something on the wall, it is much more satisfying to seek out prints and paintings of subjects that interest you and group them together in an imaginative way.

T he idea of grouping pictures on a wall according to a particular theme that interests you is very appealing. It immediately suggests that you want the group to be viewed as a whole, and together the pictures command more attention than if they were displayed in solitary splendour.

Animals and plants are particularly rich sources of picture material. Within the natural world there is something to suit all tastes from the cute and pretty to the wild and fantastic. Animal lovers can hunt down flocks of birds or shoals of fish to hang together on a wall, while plant fanciers can root round for herbaceous borders full of paintings, prints or engravings of fruits, flowers and leaves.

Since the very earliest cave paintings, artists and illustrators have interpreted the natural world in many different ways, producing everything from perfectly lifelike portraits to highly stylized and cartoon representations of wildlife. In your displays, you can either concentrate on the regularity and similarity of frames and images, or deliberately go for frames with different shapes and colours and diverse styles of artwork to create more eclectic groupings.

Groups of pictures have a way of growing, as you add more images to your arrangement. You can even create links between the pictures in a group with a stencilled design, cord or ribbon. However, don't let a group get too large, or it starts to look straggly.

Honours are evenly divided in this display between two birds, two fish and two farm animals. It's a very collectable group of colourful prints that could grow and grow.

◀ *The most successful picture groupings* have a definite pattern to their layout. Here, for example, different sizes and styles of floral studies are ranged very effectively round the head of a bed.

▲ *Making the frames*, rather than the images they encase, the focus of attention is an equally effective approach to arranging pictures. Here, the frames are many and varied, while the photocopied engravings of flowers and leaves are relatively low-key.

▲ *Perched symmetrically in place* above the fireplace, two bird prints reinforce the rich and slightly formal tones of the room. The choice of the strong brown mountboard for the prints acts as a balance to the deep timber of the mantelpiece below.

▶ *Plump peaches*, pears and apples, carefully depicted in rich red and golden tones, are in keeping with the understated elegance of this room. The wide, white mounts and bird's-eye maple frames set the prints off well against the pale walls.

SUSPENSE STORIES

Fine tune your picture collection by suspending each image with a series of pert bows, lengths of silken cord or swags of soft chiffon. The trim can be highly functional or purely decorative.

F or a finishing flourish to a room, hang up your prints and pictures in an inventive way. The method you employ can be as simple as a grosgrain ribbon, twisted into a discreet bow and used to frame the picture, or as flamboyant as a drape of dreamy muslin, falling well below the base of the picture itself. It is a great way of linking a series of mismatched images, or making a simple print look more interesting.

On the whole the easiest way to achieve the effect is to hang up the picture in the conventional way, using a basic hook fixed to the wall behind. The device that you use to decorate it

can then be more unexpected. There is no need, for instance, for a picture bow to take the weight of the picture – it can be suspended from a decorative hook positioned just above the picture and, if you allow the tails to hang below the picture, it will look like the main support.

If a picture bow can work in this way, why not try a less conventional means of support? A long silken scarf, for example, provides a fragile, softening touch as it slithers down the wall behind the picture. To add textural impact, try twisting ropes of decorator's cord or even raffia together in a number of strong colours.

A picture rail provides the obvious means of support for this symmetrical arrangement – yet the cord used to hang the picture is far from conventional. It becomes an important part of the total display and helps to link the composition.

95

◤ *Creamy grosgrain ribbon adds grace to these understated botanical prints. The ribbon, cut and stitched into a flat bow and suspended from a dainty picture hook, is strong enough to take the weight of the print. The brass picture hook is a clever touch, as it subtly echoes the glinting gold of the frame.*

◀ *The bold bow, in this case, is of prime importance to the overall image. It repeats the fabric used as a backing for the daffodil print and, courtesy of its large scale, it adds the missing element of drama to what would otherwise be a very simple image.*

▲ *Lengths of strong wire, looped over the top of the picture rail and attached to the back of each framed print, provide imaginative, but not intrusive, support.*

▶ *Swathes of muslin, suspended from gilded mouldings and linking the rows of pictures, add a softening touch to a formal display. The muslin is purely decorative – the pictures are supported by picture hooks.*

DISPLAYING PLATES

When it comes to adding instant interest to a bare stretch of wall, pretty plates, grouped together in clusters, displayed singly or hung in horizontal or vertical rows, are an innovative option.

anging decorative plates makes a pleasant change from, or addition to, conventional paintings, prints or posters. It's also a more immediate and economical project – the chances are you already have some plates worth hanging. Porcelain, china, earthenware or glass, glazed or unglazed, highly decorated or plain – whatever looks right in the room is fine.

Souvenir plates are designed to be hung on walls but there's no need to stop there. Antique shops often have beautiful but reasonably priced plates with barely visible hairline cracks or chips which make them unsuitable for normal use but ideal for wall display. For fun on a budget, collect and hang antique saucers, since these often remain once their cups are broken and, again, are relatively inexpensive. And because they are small, you can display several in a modest space. If you can't run to genuine antiques, many manufacturers do excellent reproductions

Try to relate the display to furniture, such as above a sofa, or hang plates above a fireplace or door, on a narrow wall between two doors or windows or just under the ceiling, like a wall frieze.

Play safe with valuable plates – display them on plate stands on a shelf rather than hanging them from a wall. Clip-on wire holders are fine for plates that aren't too precious, but if you want to avoid scratching the plate use a special adhesive pad and ring stuck to the back of the plate.

A mixed medley of old-fashioned blue and white plates forms a flower-like focal point, reflecting the colour scheme of the bedlinen.

⬛ *A single plate* topped by a coordinating bow adds cheer to any wall. Consider hanging a fun plate like this in a bathroom – unlike a poster or print, it won't be damaged by steamy conditions.

⬛ *Enlivening a wall,* green glazed serving plates with Victorian-style sculptured motifs link the Victorian wall tiles and fruit bowl below with the row of green mugs above. The overall effect is one of quiet restraint, in keeping with the kitchen's simple decor.

⬛ *Ribbon laced round* a filigree rim turns an inexpensive plate into an eye-catching wall display. A glass plate is ideal on patterned wallpaper like this, as the floral design shows through to enhance the effect.

⬛ *A trio of plates* linked by a tasselled cord make a fine display. Plates don't have to match to work well together – these three came from diverse sources but they team up nicely as they share a botanical theme.

FRAMED REFLECTIONS

*A plain mirror becomes a new focus of attention when you
add a highly textured frame, which you can make for yourself from
surprisingly inexpensive materials.*

Plain mirrors are a quick, economical way to add interest to a wall but they are also essentially neutral, fairly anonymous objects. You can easily give a mirror a unique and memorable character by making a customized textured frame for it. It is very effective for large mirrors situated in key positions, such as above a mantelpiece. Mirrors that merge into the surrounding background also benefit from decorative frames.

The key to creating a unique mirror frame is in picking suitable objects to stick on to the frame. For a collage-type effect, choose small, lightweight objects with an overall, unifying theme. For a child's mirror, for example, try tiny toys, brightly coloured pencils, crayons or jigsaw puzzle pieces. To decorate a kitchen mirror, try dried pasta, pulses, varnished dough sculpture or dried herbs and spices. Use sparkling sequin strips to create a Hollywood-type fantasy mirror frame for a star-struck teenager; or nuts, bolts and screws for a humorous, masculine effect.

You can decorate just the top of the mirror, continue the decorations partway down the sides or completely cover the frame. Try emphasizing the top section with larger or more elaborate decorations. For an informal effect, let the decorations overlap the surface of the mirror. Place the mirror on a flat surface and experiment with where you want the objects before sticking them on to the frame.

Dried flowers, grains, seed pods, nuts, fungi and spices in natural colours adorn this mantelpiece mirror to make a really attractive frame.

Simple and substantial, this frame of solid, weather-worn timber is ideal for a rustic setting, combining well with golden, earthy tones. When you find the right frame for the location, all the embellishment it needs is a good clean and perhaps a lick of varnish or paint.

Mother-of-pearl buttons, in various shapes and sizes, give a simple white frame a delicate, feminine look. Decorating only two corners helps to draw attention to the detail of the shimmering buttons and softens the rigid edges of the frame.

A shell-encrusted mirror frame emphasizes this bathroom's marine theme, and provides subtle variations on its soft beige tones. The frame features symmetrical clusters of shells and large shells in each corner for a formal effect.

Fabric roses and artificial foliage combine to create a pretty garland for this table-top mirror. The floral fabric matches the wallpaper, for a designer touch.

STYLISH PIN-UPS

*A pinboard can do more than help you organize your busy
lifestyle – it can also become an eye-catching display point for favourite nick-
nacks and mementoes which you want to keep on view.*

Pinboards are no longer being relegated to the backs of doors or dingy kitchen corners – they're stepping out of the shadows and becoming stylish accessories worthy of a prime spot in the home. A stroll around your local department store or stationery shop reveals lots of pinboard options – from novelty, children's designs decorated in bright colours and featuring lovable cartoon characters, to smart, fabric-covered boards with neat criss-crossing braids and glass-headed pins. And if you can't find a pinboard that's right for you, it's easy to make your own, or to customize a cheap shop-bought board with paints, decorative mouldings and braid or ribbon trims.

Once you've chosen a pinboard you like, and which suits your decor, you'll be happy to hang it where it should be hung – in a prominent place. Give it added appeal by making it into a personalized display piece, showing more than just the usual collection of phone numbers, bills and shopping lists. Pin on attractive postcards, favourite photos, even small nick-nacks and mementoes to add interest to the board. The beauty of pinboards is that you can alter their contents with ease whenever you feel like a change. Have a thorough clear-out of the board regularly, to stop it becoming too cluttered. Young and old are drawn to its bright and sparkling myriad of colours and designs.

This framed, fabric-covered pinboard makes a lively background against which to display colourful cards and nick-nacks. You can either pin items in place, or slip them behind the board's criss-crossing braids.

▶ A magnificent gilded frame makes an appropriately handsome surround for a pinboard bearing fine art prints and treasured mementoes from times past. The board's location, just over the kitchen sink, makes washing up a more pleasurable pastime.

◥ Dedicated wine drinkers can at last find a use for all those bottle corks – glue them on to a piece of plywood to create a kitchen pinboard with a difference. Stick the corks with any print facing outwards, so they'll remind you of favourite wines enjoyed over the years.

◢ Criss-crossing yellow ricrac braid transforms this old, baize-covered pinboard into a jazzy accessory for a child's room. The ricrac cross-points are secured to the front of the board with brass upholstery nails, passed through bright scraps of felt.

◀ You can now buy the ultimate in chic, fabric-covered pinboards from some soft-furnishing stockists to coordinate with their ranges.

PLATE SHELVES

Plate shelves are a great way to keep attractive pottery on display, while storing it tidily and safely out of harm's way – and you can still easily reach up and take an item when you want to use it.

P late shelves fixed high up on the wall take up much less room than a dresser or shelf unit, but can hold just as much if you extend them right round the room. Use them in a dual role – as platforms for displaying favourite crockery and ornaments and for relatively easy-access storage.

A plate shelf is usually fixed at picture rail height, but you can position it lower if you require frequent access to the items it carries. Avoid fixing it at eye level and site it out of the way, where you won't bang your head on it or knock items off as you brush past. Over work surfaces is an ideal spot in the kitchen, especially if you're using the shelf to store cooking ingredients, such as flour, pasta, pulses and herbs – they'll be right at your fingertips. Likewise, in the bathroom a

narrow plate shelf fixed at dado height and extending round the bath is perfect for storing everyday toiletries. Decant bath oils, lotions and cleansers into elegant bottles, and store kitchen ingredients in stylish glass or ceramic jars, to make an attractive display on the shelf.

You can buy plate shelves in easy-to-assemble kit form or as mouldings, or you can make your own. If you want to display plates, the shelves need to have a groove cut into them to hold the plate rims. Alternatively, you can add a shelf edge trim to prevent the plates sliding off. Make sure you fix the shelves securely in place, as they may have to carry a fair bit of weight. Finish them with paint, stain or varnish to match the decor.

A wide plate shelf fixed over a kitchen-dining table makes an easily accessible storage spot for a plate rack, set of scales and various containers; it also enhances the snug feel of this cosy corner by breaking up the wall space.

◪ *A plate shelf fixed high up on the wall* provides a safe haven for a decorative display of blue-and-white treasures. Note how the curtain pole is slotted neatly into two specially adapted shelf brackets.

◪ *Two-tier plate shelves* running across two walls of this kitchen area provide extensive storage space, while allowing carefully coordinated crockery and neat jars of ingredients to remain on view and accessible. Cups and herbs hang from useful hooks screwed into the bottom shelf.

▸ *As you recline in this bath,* all your toiletries are close to hand. A narrow plate shelf fixed round the bath at about dado height is just the thing for holding attractively packaged soaps and bath oils.

PLASTER COVING

*You can add instant elegance and character to a room
by decorating the junction between walls and ceiling with distinctive strips of
coving made from traditional plaster or modern synthetic polystyrene.*

Decorative plaster coving or deeper, more elaborate cornicing softens the transition between the wall and the ceiling. At the same time, it can conceal uneven joins and also hide any harmless but unsightly cracks that often form in the junction between the wall and ceiling as the house settles.

Before selecting a design, it is worth considering which width and pattern suits the scale and style of your room best. Plain, narrow concave strips of coving provide a neat trim at ceiling level; more ornate plaster mouldings, depicting stylized leaves, flowers or geometric designs like Greek key patterns, introduce an appealing period feel to a room. Depending on how much of a feature you want to make of the coving, you can paint it to contrast with the colour of the wall or ceiling, or to coordinate with it.

Concave gypsum plaster coving, covered with embossed cove border, is a smart way to finish off the junction between walls and ceiling. The fluted corner pieces simplify fitting and add to the decorative effect.

PUTTING UP COVING

Plan the layout of the coving or cornice carefully before you begin, so that you don't have to join lengths in visible areas of the room. Generally, begin fixing the moulding in a corner of the longest wall facing you as you come into the room. Try to avoid fitting small sections, where two adjacent seams are hard to hide.

Set up a working platform so that you can reach the ceiling easily. Planks laid between two decorator's trestles are safer than working from a stepladder. Long lengths of plaster coving are heavy while polystyrene coving is unwieldy; an extra pair of hands makes fitting much easier. Carry the lengths of cornice carefully between the two of you. Hold the top edge and carry it on edge; don't carry a long section flat in case it sags and cracks.

Covings are styled with a flat face at the top and back to fit tightly against the ceiling and wall. They are stuck in place with a special plaster or polystyrene coving adhesive. Use rustproof nails as well as adhesive to hold heavy fibrous plaster coving.

You can cut polystyrene coving with a sharp carving knife but you should use a fine toothed tenon saw to cut plaster coving. Gypsum plaster and polystyrene cornerpieces are available to avoid the need for cutting mitred corners.

FITTING GYPSUM PLASTER COVING

If you decide not to use cornerpieces, you need to mitre the ends of the coving in a mitre box. You can either use the guidelines on the ceiling for marking up internal corners and the wall for external ones, or look out for plaster coving that comes with a template to make cutting mitred corners easier. You simply trace the shape of the corners on to the coving with a pencil, and cut along the guideline with a craft knife or saw.

Don't worry too much about perfect seams and mitres, as you can fill gaps at corners and joins, or between coving and wall or ceiling, with fine-surface plaster filler. You can get gypsum plaster cove corners to fit over existing mitred corners later on if you wish.

> ### YOU WILL NEED
>
> - ❖ PENCIL AND TAPE MEASURE
> - ❖ GYPSUM PLASTER COVING
> - ❖ MITRE BOX
> - ❖ FINE-TOOTHED TENON SAW OR CRAFT KNIFE
> - ❖ STRAIGHTEDGE
> - ❖ PLASTER COVING ADHESIVE
> - ❖ ADHESIVE SPREADER
> - ❖ GALVANIZED NAILS AND HAMMER
> - ❖ FINE-SURFACE PLASTER FILLER
> - ❖ FILLING KNIFE

1 Drawing guidelines Ensure that the wall and ceiling surfaces are clean, smooth and dry. Then hold a small piece of coving in place at the starting corner. Mark pencil guidelines on the ceiling and wall along the top and bottom of the coving. Continue marking in the same way all round the room. To give the coving a good grip, lightly score the area between the guidelines with a craft knife.

2 Measuring up Measure the length of each wall between corners – at external corners allow for an overlap of at least one coving's width. Cut to length with a fine-toothed tenon saw or craft knife.

3 Marking internal corners With a friend, carefully lift a length of coving up to the wall and push it tightly into the first corner. In pencil, mark on the top edge where the coving crosses the guideline on the ceiling. Mark the adjoining piece of coving in the same way on the adjacent wall.

4 Marking an external corner Hold a length of coving up to the wall and, with a pencil, mark off the end of the wall on its lower edge. Without moving the coving, then mark where the top edge intersects the guideline on the ceiling. Repeat for the coving on the other side of the corner.

▼▼▼ **TIP** ▼▼▼

DECORATING COVING

You can buy an embossed cove border to add colour and pattern to the plain gypsum plaster coving. You simply use a wallpaper adhesive to stick it along the concave face of the coving. If you like you can add another strip over or under the dado rail to achieve a comprehensively moulded look.

5 Cutting the mitre Lay the coving on its back on the floor. Using a straightedge and pencil, draw a diagonal line from the marked point on the top edge to the lower corner for an internal corner, or between the two marked points on the top and lower edges for an external one. Put the cornice in a mitre box and cut along the marked lines. Then lift two pieces up to the corner at the same time to check the join.

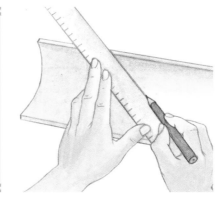

6 Fixing the coving Spread adhesive along the flat surfaces on the back of the first length of coving. Press it firmly but gently against the wall and ceiling and push the pointed lower edge into the corner. Make sure the coving grips the wall along its top and bottom edges. With a damp cloth, wipe away any adhesive that squeezes out from behind the coving. To hold it in place until the adhesive sets, knock a few nails into the wall at regular intervals under the lower edge.

7 Fitting the remaining coving Spread adhesive on the adjacent lengths of coving and press them into position in the same way to form neat butt joins. Continue fitting the rest of the coving round the room.

8 Hiding the joins When the adhesive is set, remove the supporting nails and fill the holes in the wall and any gaps between the joins with fine-surface plaster filler, smoothing it in with your fingertip. Leave to dry before painting the coving.

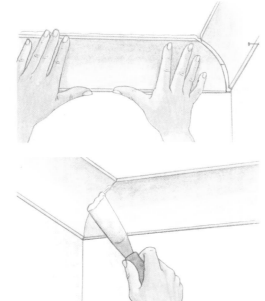

▲ *Shaped plaster coving and an equally plain ceiling centrepiece add a tasteful elegance to a simply decorated room. The corresponding cornerpieces make mitre joints redundant.*

FIBROUS PLASTER COVE

The procedure for measuring up, cutting and mitring traditional fibrous plaster coving is identical to fitting the gypsum plaster type except that you need to knock some galvanized nails through the coving itself into the wall and the joists in the ceiling to hold it permanently. Use a nail punch to bury the nail heads under the plaster and fill with fine-surface filler when tidying up the corners and joins.

FIXING POLYSTYRENE COVING

Polystyrene is the simplest of all coving types to put up, because it is so light and manageable. You just have to be careful not to push your fingers or nails through the soft polystyrene when you are pressing it to the wall and ceiling. Polystyrene moulding covered with paper is more robust but just as lightweight.

To avoid creating a serious fire hazard, always use emulsion paint for decorating polystyrene coving; never paint over it with gloss paint.

YOU WILL NEED

- ❖ **POLYSTYRENE COVING AND CORNERPIECES**
- ❖ **PENCIL AND TAPE MEASURE**
- ❖ **KITCHEN KNIFE OR FINE-TOOTHED TENON SAW**
- ❖ **STRAIGHTEDGE**
- ❖ **POLYSTYRENE COVING ADHESIVE**
- ❖ **ADHESIVE SPREADER**

1 Preparing the surfaces Prepare the walls and ceiling and mark in the guidelines as for steps 1 and 2, *Fitting Gypsum Plaster Coving.*

2 Fitting cornerpieces Fix all the cornerpieces before fitting the straight pieces. Spread plenty of adhesive along the flat back and top edges of the first cornerpiece and press it firmly but gently into position in the corner.

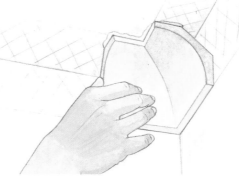

▲ *A cornerpiece with an embossed Greek key design is a decorative way of joining two straight lengths of plain polystyrene coving at a corner.*

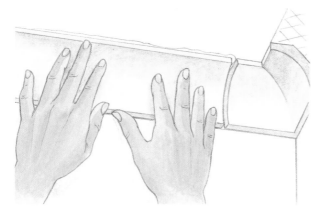

3 Cutting the coving to fit Measure the length of each wall between cornerpieces. If necessary, using a kitchen knife and a steel straightedge, cut straight across the coving to make it fit. Glue straight pieces along the walls, butting up the ends to the cornerpieces and each other. Scrape away excess adhesive that squeezes out from under the coving with a filling knife and use it to neaten the joins.

▶ *Pre-mitred external and internal corner sets to match paper-covered polystyrene coving save having to cut the mitres yourself. Plain polystyrene coving comes with embossed cornerpieces that serve the same purpose. You can paint both sorts with emulsion paint to complement the rest of the room.*

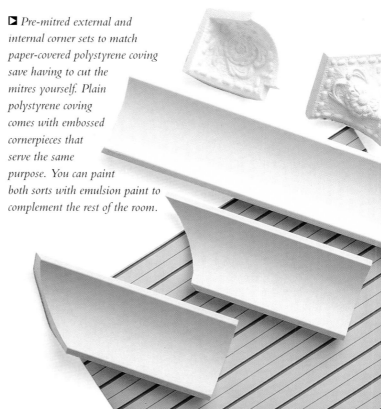

CHOOSING CERAMIC TILES

Tiles come in many different shapes and sizes, and in thousands of colours and patterns. Once fixed, tiling is semi-permanent, so it is wise to be sure of your choice before you buy.

Hardwearing, waterproof and easy to clean, ceramic tiles are the perfect choice for kitchen and bathroom walls, where steam and airborne grease from cooking can soon damage wallcoverings or paint. Tiles can also find a place in the living areas of the home, especially on hall walls and in the conservatory. Ceramic wall tiles are available in many different shapes and sizes and in thousands of colours and patterns. Prices range from budget to expensive, depending on whether you choose a mass produced or a handmade design.

Mass produced tiles are either completely flat or have a slightly textured surface; patterns are machine printed, so colours are even throughout.

Mass-produced tiles are made with slightly bevelled edges and come in various thicknesses.

Handmade tiles are individually moulded, so the surface is often slightly bumpy and the edges may not be completely straight, making them a little trickier to put up. Colours and the depth of glaze vary, giving a pleasing rustic effect. Again, thickness also varies.

Reproduction tiles, manufactured using Victorian techniques, are expensive but a good choice if you want to create a Victorian-style hallway or conservatory, or replace missing decoration on a period fireplace. Colours are rich and deep, and the decoration has an embossed appearance.

As well as being a practical choice, tiles can add character to any room in the house. These handpainted animal tiles introduce colour and humour to a wash basin splashback.

WALL TILE TYPES

General purpose wall tiles, or field tiles, are designed to be used alone or with coordinating tiles in a complementary pattern or colour. They are available in both manufactured and hand-made ranges. You can choose from a large selection of plain colours, or a design with an all over pattern. Some handmade tiles have a crackle-glaze finish, to give an antiqued look.

Tile sizes vary from 25mm (1in) to 600mm (24in) square. They also come in rectangular sizes.

Worktop tiles are available in both mass produced and handmade ranges and are sold with curved pieces to be used between the worktop and the wall and along the front edge. Never cover a worktop with ordinary wall tiles: they are not strong enough to stand the impact of thermal shock from hot pans, and may craze or fade if you use a household cleaner on the surface. If you are going to tile your worktops, it's a good idea to inset a marble or slate slab, or a wooden chopping block, for food preparation.

Patterned or **decor tiles** come in the same selection of sizes as general purpose tiles, and can be mixed with them at random or used in a more formal way. The pattern on handmade relief decor tiles stands proud of the surface of the tile. Decor tiles are available in a single design or a set of several different tiles with the same decorative theme, such as a selection of fruit, flowers or country scenes.

Special shaped tiles are available in addition to the standard square and rectangular wall tile shapes. These include diamond, triangular, cross, honeycomb and other shapes. They can be used alone, or combined with square or rectangular shapes to create interesting designs.

Tile panels are available in some tile ranges. These are picture panels made up of four or more decorated tiles. Small, four tile pictures can be dotted within a large expanse of plain tiled wall. Larger, more complex pictures work well as a focal point: behind a hob, on the wall beside the bath, or as a wash basin splashback.

Mosaic tiles are made from small chips of coloured stone or ceramic and are a good choice for the bathroom, or for a conservatory. Individual mosaic pieces are available and can look attractive set into concrete or plaster, but work the design out on graph paper before you start.

If you want to cover a large area, choose mosaic tiles where many small pieces are mounted on a flexible backing.

▶ *Creative framing*
Mass produced tiles in pale sea green and white provide a soothing colour scheme for a bathroom. A patterned frame prevents too clinical an effect.

*To add a focal point to a plain
expanse of field tiles, consider a
picture panel such as this spring tulip
display. Choose from the same range
as your field tiles, or ensure all tiles
are the same size and thickness.*

◀ Mosaic effect

*Mosaic-style tiles in three shades of blue
conjure up images of the sea and break up a
large expanse of wall.*

▶ Adding interest

*Plain white tiles are enlivened with a border
frame and matching inset patterned tiles.*

Border tiles are useful for finishing off an
edge halfway up a wall or for dividing plain
and patterned tiling.

Full size border tiles, usually found in
mass produced ranges, have a border pattern
printed across the upper section and can be
used in the middle of a wall, to divide plain
and pattern, or at the top.

Narrow border tiles are the same width as
general purpose or decor tiles but about
76mm (3in) deep, and can be used to finish a
line of tiling, or to divide a large area. Relief
borders have raised decoration.

Dado tiles are a ceramic version of the
wooden dado rail and are usually found in
more expensive ranges. The tiles are always
plain, but sometimes embossed, and are used
to divide or top coordinated plain or patterned general purpose field tiles.

Listello or **slip tiles** are long, narrow tiles,
which are either flat or rounded. They are
found in Victorian or Edwardian ranges and
can be used above or below the dado to
create a deeper border. Alternatively, you can
use a row of listello tiles between plain and
patterned field tiles before finishing off
with a dado.

Buying Tips

❖ **Choose with care** – tiling is semi-permanent decoration. Removal is difficult and may involve replastering the wall beneath.

❖ **Consider the scale** – generally speaking, it's a good idea to use small tiles for small expanses of wall, and larger tiles where there is more space. Large tiles on a small section of wall look odd and usually involve a great deal of cutting. Small tiles can make a large area seem cluttered and, because more are needed, will probably be dearer (and certainly more time-consuming) than using a larger tile.

❖ **Take samples home** – never buy new tiles without taking several different types home, so that you can see how the colour or pattern looks with your kitchen furniture or bathroom suite.

And remember that colours can appear dramatically different under shop lighting. Look at the tiles in the room where they will be used, in both natural and artificial light, before making a final colour choice.

❖ **Special measurements** – if you plan to use decor tiles, mark crosses on the wall where they will be positioned, and count the number to see how many you need to buy. For border tiles, measure the width of the area. If you plan to use two different tiles divided by a border or dado, measure the two areas separately.

❖ **Buy sale or return** – never underestimate the amount of tiles you'll need, but as tiles are expensive, ask if it's possible to buy on a sale or return basis. Most DIY stores and tile shops will give credit for whole unused boxes.

◢ *Animal motif*
Raised pattern tiles such as these frogs are a fun way of adding interest to plain tiles.

◢ *Colour gradation*
The tiles from some ranges have an interesting gradation of colour not only from tile to tile but within individual tiles themselves. Colours vary from box to box within the same range – for a good blend of colours mix up tiles from different boxes.

◀ *Victorian panel*
Victorian tiles can often be picked up in junk shops. Alternatively, there are many good modern reproductions. Build up a collection of favourites to create a multi-coloured panel for your wall.

▼ *Fireplace tiles*
This modern version of a late Victorian design is repeated in the hearth, and makes the fireplace eyecatching even during the summer months. Special fireplace tiles are made to withstand extreme heat.

▲ *Diagonal style*
Rows of different patterned tiles from the same handpainted Mexican range look effective when laid diagonally.

113

DESIGN IDEAS

❖ **Spread the cost** by mixing expensive handpainted decor tiles with cheaper, mass produced plain field tiles – but make sure before you buy that the two different types are the same thickness.

❖ **Original Victorian** or **Dutch Delft** decorated tiles can sometimes be found in antique shops, and look effective dotted around a wall of plain white tiling. Alternatively, build up a collection of antique tiles and use them to make a splashback for a wash basin, or as a focal point panel behind a hob or cooker top or on a straight wall. To achieve a similar effect at less expense, look for good quality reproductions of traditional tiles.

❖ **Be creative with shapes** – small, square tiles look effective laid diagonally, especially if you use several toning shades of the same colour. Or experiment by laying the tiles in a diamond formation to create an interesting border or dividing line. Cut whole tiles in half to fill the triangular gaps.

❖ **Make a border** by cutting contrasting or toning plain tiles in half diagonally. Laid together, the triangles make an attractive border or divider at far less expense than buying special border tiles.

❖ **Create your own picture panels** by framing an area with narrow border tiles. Dot decor tiles around within the tiled frame, or for a subtle effect fill the framed area with tiles in a darker or paler colour.

🔺 *Building up borders*
The effect of these handsome terracotta pavers is enhanced with an inset border of diagonally laid whole and half tiles.

🔻 *Tile style*
Field and border tiles come in a range of plain colours and modern and traditional designs.

🔺 *Colour blend*
An apparently random selection of colours from the same tile range can create a wonderful blend of colours, such as the warm earth tones of the large tiles used in this shower room.

Tiling Walls

Tiles have a decorative quality unmatched by any other wall finish. Not only do they look good, they are immensely practical, hardwearing and waterproof too.

There are plenty of good reasons for extending a tiled area beyond a small splashback behind a basin or sink. In many bathrooms, condensation alone plays havoc with wallpaper and if you have a shower or children who enjoy splashing around you definitely need a waterproof finish on the walls. In kitchens, tiles also provide an easy-to-clean surface behind worktops and stoves. While tiles can work out to be an expensive option, they are durable and will provide long-lasting style.

The key to achieving a professional finish is to plan the job from beginning to end before you even buy your tiles. Knowing the tricks of the trade for dealing with awkward areas makes the world of difference between a first-class and an indifferent finish; as does planning ahead for the discreet positioning of any cut tiles. Working your way through the job on paper highlights these areas, allows you to experiment at no cost and more than repays the time spent in the long run.

Ceramic tiles are an attractive and practical way to decorate a wall in a kitchen or bathroom. They're easy to clean, waterproof and very hardwearing, and there are designs to suit all tastes and decors.

SETTING OUT

Setting out is the first stage of putting your tiling plan into action. Doing this properly ensures that cut tiles fall neatly on either side of the area to be tiled and that your tiles are positioned squarely. This is of critical importance to achieving a good finish.

Normally you fit tiles working upwards from the edge of a bath, the rim of a shower tray, a kitchen worktop, the top of a skirting board or the floor, all of which are likely to be too uneven to use as a base. So your first job is to draw a horizontal baseline which ensures that every row of tiles is level. Then you fix a straight batten along this line to support the first row of tiles.

You also need to set the width of the end columns on either side of the tiled area. Mark out each wall so that as far as possible you avoid cut tiles at external corners and at the sides of windows. Where cuts are required at both ends of a wall, find its midpoint and measure out from here so that each end column is even and, preferably, not less than half a tile in width.

HOW MANY TILES?

Find the area in square metres of each surface to be covered by multiplying its height by its width. Add the areas together and multiply by the number of tiles of your chosen design it takes to cover a square metre – this information is generally supplied on the packaging. Allow an extra five per cent for wastage.

If you have an exposed edge or edges to your tiling area, make sure you have enough suitable edging tiles, with rounded or glazed edges, unless you are using angled, universal tiles or fitting an edge trim.

1 Marking a guideline Using a straightedge and spirit level, draw a line right round the bottom of the area to be tiled, approximately a tile's width above where the lowest tiles are to finish.

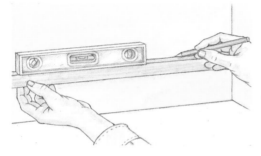

2 Drawing the baseline Take one tile and, holding it level with the base of the area to be tiled, mark the point where it rises highest above the guideline. Add 3mm (⅛in) to allow for the width of a grout line and draw the baseline round the bottom of the area to be tiled at this height, parallel to the guideline.

3 Fitting the support battens At 30cm (1ft) intervals, partly drive masonry nails into lengths of batten so that the points just show through. Position the top edge of one length of batten along the baseline and drive the nails into the wall until they hold, but no further than necessary – you will need to remove the batten later. Continue fitting battens along the baseline.

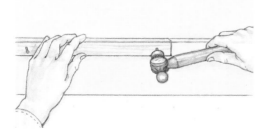

4 Positioning the end columns With your marking stick, work out where the last columns of whole tiles end on either side. Use a plumb line to draw vertical lines at these points.

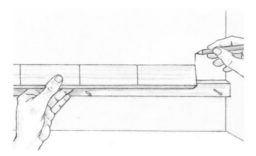

5 Fitting vertical battens Fix further lengths of batten, at right angles to the first, along the outside of the vertical lines, as in step 3. Check that the battens are vertical with a spirit level.

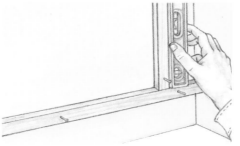

FITTING THE TILES

The tiles are fitted in horizontal rows from the bottom of the area to be tiled upwards. Work over a small area of the wall at a time so the tile adhesive does not dry out before you have a chance to embed the tiles.

1 Fitting the first row Spread about 1 sq m (1 sq yd) of tiling adhesive on the wall, using a notched spreader to leave it in ridges. Fix the first tile in the corner of the two battens. Continue fitting the tiles building up three or four rows at a time. With square-edged tiles, bed plastic spacers in the adhesive between the tiles; for tiles with angled edges or spacer lugs, push them up against one another.

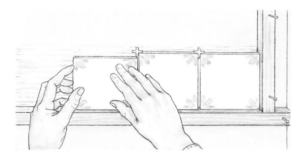

2 Releasing the battens Continue applying blocks of adhesive and tiles between the battens. Leave to set for an hour, then slide a knife blade along the batten edges to clear the joints. Remove the battens by pulling out the nails with pincers. Measure and cut tiles to fit the gaps and then fix them in place with tile adhesive.

◥ *A simple chequerboard pattern of yellow and deep green tiles is an effective choice for the walls of a utility room.*

3 Grouting the tiles Leave the tiles to set, usually for 12 hours. Cover the surrounding area. Apply and finish the grout and seal any gaps along the adjoining bath edge, shower tray or worktop with sealant.

◀ *Topiary trees are the unusual subject for the tiles of this kitchen splashback. Using a border tile means that two complete tiles fit in each vertical row, while a third tile needs a little cutting to fill in the gap under the dish-drying rack.*

Positioning a band of border tiles at window level all round the room enhances the proportions of the whole room. The edges of the window recess are neatened with a double-edge trim strip. Tiling the deep windowsill provides an extra storage surface.

CUTTING TILES

Generally, on a run of tiles along a wall, you will need to cut the tiles at each end to fit the area. When tiling a bath surround or the area behind a kitchen worktop, there should be no need for anything other than straight cuts which are quite simple to make.

A tile-cutting jig is the best way to make straight cuts parallel to the sides of the tiles. The jig has a built-in marking gauge which you set to the width of the gap to be filled before cutting; it automatically allows for the width of one grout line.

However, because a tile-cutting jig can only hold the tile to be cut squarely, you cannot use it to score diagonal cuts on the tile. To fill slanting gaps, you have to mark the tile by hand with a felt-tip pen, then score it with a handheld tile cutter against a straightedge.

1 Sizing up the cut Check that the space for a cut tile is uniform by measuring it top and bottom using the jig. If it is, you can use the jig to cut the tile. If not, transfer the measurements directly to the tile and make allowance for the grout line.

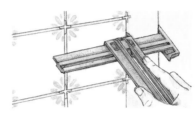

2 Cutting the tile *In a jig:* position the tile in the jig. Holding the tile and jig steady with one hand, line up the tile cutting tool in the guide and draw it firmly along the slot towards you. *By hand:* to cut a tile to fit a non-uniform gap, join the marks on the tile with a ruler and felt-tip pen. Use a hand cutter along a metal straightedge to score the tile surface.

3 Splitting the tile Grip the tile between the jaws of the cutting tool, with the jaws directly over the scored line. Hold the free side of the tile with your other hand, and squeeze gently with the tool to snap. Check the fit and smooth the cut edge with a tile file.

TILING CORNERS

Almost every tiling job involves turning a corner at some point. Prepare yourself for tackling corners during your planning and setting out.

Fitting into internal corners At internal corners, overlap one set of cut edges on to another. Plan in advance which way to arrange the overlap, and allow for a grout line.

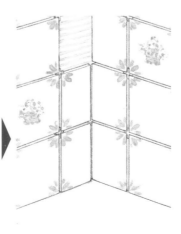

Fitting round external corners (1) You can finish external corners with a double-edge trim strip. Bed the strip in the adhesive, then simultaneously fix both columns of tiles so you can align them. You can use a single-edge trim strip for finishing off an exposed edge to a tiled area, especially when using plain-edged tiles.

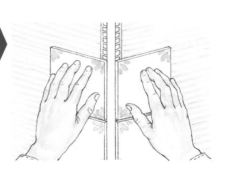

Fitting round external corners (2) Instead of using trim strip, overlap the adjacent tiles, making sure that the overlapping edge is glazed or rounded.

Wall tiling essentials

Ceramic tiles make an attractive, long-lasting covering for bathroom and kitchen walls.

With the right tools and materials, and careful planning and preparation, tiling a smooth, level wall is a straightforward job. The equipment needed for tiling is readily available from DIY stores. Always work in a well ventilated room when tiling, and wear gloves when handling grout and adhesive if your skin is at all sensitive.

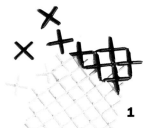

1

Tiling tools and materials

Tile adhesive sticks the tiles to the wall and comes ready to use in tubs. Check the tub for how much you will need. There are various kinds. Standard PVA based adhesives are only partly water resistant but are quite suitable for most walls and basin or sink splashbacks. Water resistant, acrylic-based adhesives are more expensive but are best for shower cubicles and bath splashbacks. Heat resistant adhesives are essential where temperatures are unusually high, such as around fires and cookers.

A notched adhesive spreader (3) furrows the adhesive, ensuring an even thickness. Sometimes one is supplied with the adhesive.

Grout fills the gaps between tiles.

Ready mixed grouts are acrylic based and come in tubs.

Powder grouts, which are cement based, come in bags for mixing with water and are slightly easier to apply.

Standard grout is white, but you can buy it in a range of colours. Alternatively you can buy special grout paint. Ordinary grout is reasonably water resistant and quite suitable for showers and splashbacks, though fully water resistant grout is available.

A grout spreader (2) has a rubber blade to spread the grout into the gaps between the tiles.

A grout joint finisher is a cheap plastic tool for firming the grout into place and giving it a smooth finish. Alternatively you can use a piece of 6mm (¼in) wooden dowel or the blunt end of a round pencil.

Tile spacers (1) are small plastic crosses for spacing square edged tiles – the commonest type. Some tiles already have bevelled edges or built-in spacer lugs to create a uniform gap.

Plastic edging or finishing strip in various colours is available to round off the exposed edges of outer tiles, though some tile ranges have special border and corner tiles with glazed edges.

Plastic sealing strip gives a watertight seal where tiles join a worktop, bath or basin. It is sold in 1.8m (6ft) lengths.

Silicone or acrylic sealant in a choice of colours comes in cartridge form and is an alternative to plastic sealing strip.

A tile cutter (6) scores the glazed surface of a tile, so the tile snaps easily and cleanly along the scored line. *An all-in-one tile cutter* (8) has a lever that trims and snaps in one action.

A tile saw (7) makes curved cuts for tiling around pipes and other obstructions.

A tile file (5) smooths the edges of cut tiles.

Tile nibblers (4) whittle away strips of tile too narrow to be snapped off.

3

4

5

6

Other equipment

For a professional finish you may also need:

A length of narrow timber to use as a gauging rod. Mark tile widths plus grouting spaces on it so that you can plan the positioning of the tiles.

Two wooden battens to fix to the wall to help you position the first column and the first row of tiles accurately.

A hammer and some masonry nails to secure the battens to the wall.

A level which shows the true vertical as well as horizontal, to position the battens correctly and check the alignment of the tiles regularly.

8

7

Preparing to tile

Preparing the wall

Make sure the wall is clean, flat, dry and firm. Plywood, blockboard and plasterboard need to be properly braced so they won't flex or warp. Don't attempt to tile on hardboard – it flexes too much – or chipboard, especially in bathrooms and around kitchen sinks, because it swells when wet causing the tiles to lift. If in doubt take expert advice.

After preparing the wall, remove obstructions if possible. Shaver and power points look better if the tiling fits behind them – isolate the supply and loosen fixing screws. If necessary, get an electrician to do this.

How many tiles?

To work out how many tiles you need, find the total area by multiplying the length by the height of each of the surfaces to be tiled – remember to include window sills and reveals, and add an extra 10% for wastage. Divide the total area by the coverage area on the box of tiles to find how many boxes you need, or by the area of an individual tile.

Always buy too many rather than too few tiles – most DIY stores will give a refund if you return unopened boxes soon after purchase. It's also a good idea to buy all the tiles you think you need before you start, to avoid too great a variation in shade, and to mix the tiles in all of the boxes so you can control any slight colour variation.

Tiling on plaster

Bare plaster Run a wooden batten over the wall, mark any bumps or depressions and level them off. Allow new plaster to dry for at least a month. Seal plaster with a PVA solution.

Wallcoverings Remove all old wallcoverings, even those which are firmly stuck down. Rake out any loose plaster, fill and level the surface. Fill and level any deep cracks.

Paint Remove any flaking paint and old wallplugs, and fill any cracks and holes. Wash the wall with (sugar) soap if the paint is dirty, then rub down with wet and dry abrasive paper.

Tiling on tiles

Existing tiles are a good base for new tiling, but the old tiles must be firmly fixed and perfectly flat. To ensure new tiles will adhere well, wash the old tiles to remove grease and dirt, then score the glazed surface with a tile cutter.

Half tiled wall (A) To tile a whole wall that has been half tiled, level the two sections by having plasterboard fitted to the untiled area, and filling any gaps between the two.

Cracked tiles (B) Fill and level any superficial cracks on tiles that are firmly fixed to the wall.

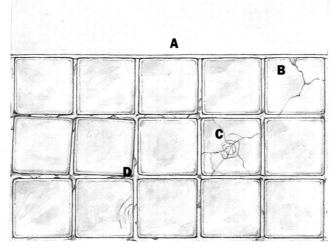

Loose tiles (D) Carefully lever off all loose tiles and either stick them – or new ones – firmly back on with tile adhesive, or level the gap with filler.

1 **Broken tiles (C) Breaking up** Tap firmly with a small hammer on a cloth pad held over the broken tile to break up the surface. To protect yourself from sharp edges you may want to wear goggles and work gloves when handling damaged tiles.

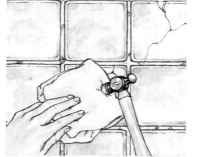

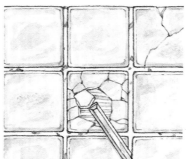

2 **Chipping out** Working from the centre outward, chip out the damaged tile with an old chisel.

TILING A SPLASHBACK

Tiling a simple splashback on the wall above a basin or sink is a perfect opportunity to try out your tiling skills. The result is a surface that looks good and is practical and long lasting.

With the help of modern tools and materials, tiling is a simple, satisfying job. If you haven't done any tiling before, a splashback is the ideal place to start, because you can get a feel for the technique without having to cut out difficult shapes.

A splashback can be a single row of tiles, or consist of several rows. Look at catalogues, magazines and shop displays to get an idea of the types of tiles available. Decide if you want plain or patterned tiles, or a mixture of both. Patterned tiles cost more, so you might opt for mainly plain tiles with a few patterned ones in groups or at random to liven them up. You can often buy small quantities of discontinued patterned tiles at a discount price, while junk shops or house clearances can be sources of beautiful old patterned tiles.

Also consider decorative border tiles, which come in many depths so you may not have to cut tiles to fit the space. Manufacturers often supply border tiles specially designed for a particular tile range, but you can choose any of the right size and thickness that you think complement the main body of the splashback.

A professional finish is within easy reach if you start with a simple project such as a splashback. Matching tiles to wallcoverings adds style, while border tiles top and bottom make for pleasing symmetry.

TILING THE EASY WAY

To be sure that your tiles stay up in place permanently and look really good, you must first take the time to prepare the wall thoroughly so that it is as clean and even as possible. You can stick tiles straight on to paint and plaster, and even on to old tiles, but not on to paper and other wallcoverings, so you must always remove these first.

After preparing the wall, work out exactly how you are going to position the tiles. Usually this means tiling outward from the middle of the wall, so that any cut tiles or gaps at the ends are the same size. Try not to use cut tiles that are less than a third of their original width. Likewise, try not to leave narrow gaps. Sit the first row of tiles against the basin if the edge is straight and level, otherwise use a wooden batten to support the first row and cut tiles to fit round the basin later.

> ### YOU WILL NEED
> ❖ TILES
> ❖ SPIRIT LEVEL
> ❖ ADHESIVE and SPREADER
> ❖ TILE SPACERS
> ❖ CLOTHS and SPONGES
> ❖ GROUT and SPREADER
> ❖ GROUT JOINT FINISHER
> ❖ SEALANT
> ❖ TILE CUTTER
> ❖ TILE FILE

▶ *The lightly patterned white tiles on this handsome kitchen sink splashback make for a happy alliance of the decorative and the functional.*

▲ *A few handpainted, floral pattern tiles scattered at random enliven a panel of plain white tiles. With fresh cut flowers to match, the overall effect is light and summery.*

POSITIONING THE TILES

Starting at the mid point
First work out the best way to position the tiles. Usually they look best laid either side of the mid point.

Centring on the mid point If starting at the mid point doesn't work, try laying out the tiles with the first one centred over the mid point instead.

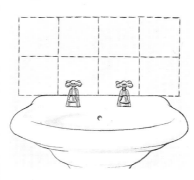

Using a batten If the back of the basin is shaped, nail a batten to the wall one tile height above the rim. Check it's level and leave nail heads protruding for easy removal. Tile above batten, then remove it and fill in base row, cutting tiles to fit.

Marking the start
Use a spirit level to draw a true vertical at the point where the tiling is to start.

STICKING THE TILES

1 **Applying the adhesive** Scoop the adhesive out of the tub and press it on to the wall. Draw the spreader across so the teeth ridge the adhesive to a level thickness. Apply enough adhesive to position up to six tiles in the first row. Make sure you can still see the mid point line – scrape away a little adhesive if necessary.

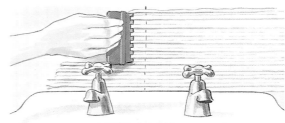

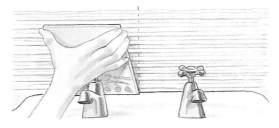

2 **Positioning the first tile** Holding the tile at an angle of 45° to the wall, align it with the vertical starting line and press it firmly back into the adhesive. Check that it is level using the spirit level.

3 **Adding further tiles** Bed spacers into the adhesive at the top and bottom of the first tile and position next tile. Continue spacing and fixing the row. Leave any cut tiles until later, but scrape off any excess adhesive before it sets.

4 **Checking the fit** Before adding further rows, check the tiles in the first row are flush with one another. Press in any that are sticking out. Prise out any that have sunk too deep and put more adhesive on the wall before rebedding them.

◀ Matching black and white accessories to border tiles shows how classy plain white tiles can be.

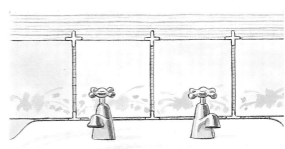

CUTTING

On a splashback there should be no need for anything other than simple straight cuts, unless the wash basin has a sculptured rim. If you have a few tiles to cut, it may be worth investing in an all-in-one cutting tool, like the one shown below, which both scores and snaps the tile – you simply position the tile carefully, score along the appropriate line, then snap the tile cleanly.

Alternatively, using a metal rule as a straight edge, score along the glazed side of the tile with a cutter, then put a matchstick under the tile along the scored line and press down firmly on both sides to snap the tile cleanly. Test the fit of each cut tile and file the cut edges smooth.

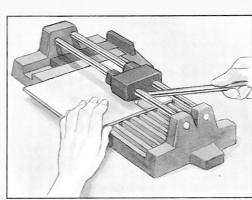

123

FINISHING OFF

When you have completed the first row of tiles you can continue sticking further rows to the wall in the same way, then leave them to set overnight before grouting the gaps.

1 Grouting the tiles Load a small amount of grout on to the flexible spreader and draw it across the gaps between the tiles, forcing it well in. Use a damp sponge to wipe off any surplus as you complete an area of about six tiles at a time.

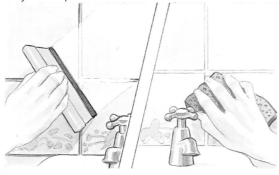

2 Finishing the joints When the grout begins to harden, smooth down the joints with a joint finisher to remove excess grout and leave the surface slightly concave.

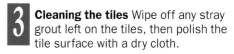 *One row of plain tiles, one row of delicately patterned tiles, chosen to blend gently with the soft tones of the bathroom, and the simplest of splashbacks is created.*

3 Cleaning the tiles Wipe off any stray grout left on the tiles, then polish the tile surface with a dry cloth.

4 Applying sealant Seal the gap along the join between the bottom row of tiles and the basin or sink with sealant. Squeeze the sealant from the tube with an even pressure and push the tube away from you along the gap. Smooth the sealant down lightly by drawing a moistened finger along the join, then leave it to set. Trim off excess sealant with a sharp blade.

◄ *Partnered by richly ornate picture tiles, plain tiles in dark colours contrast smartly with lines of white grout.*

A border of dainty gold tesserae – small mosaic squares – adds a grand flourish to this handsome mirror. The fine beading between the mirror and mosaic is gilded to match the tesserae.

MOSAIC APPEAL

Let the art of mosaic introduce rich colour and flowing pattern into your home, on walls, floors, furniture, and accessories which you can either buy or create yourself.

The art of mosaic – forming decorative designs with small pieces of glass, ceramic or any other material – has flourished for centuries: mosaic floors, walls, furniture and artefacts are to be found at many ancient sites, testifying to mosaic's strength and durability as well as its timeless appeal.

As our ancestors knew, every home benefits from the infusion of colour and pattern that mosaic decoration brings – whether over whole walls and floors, as splashbacks, friezes or worksurfaces, or to embellish furniture and accessories such as table tops, lampbases, mirror and picture frames.

You'll find a range of mosaic items in shops, but it is highly satisfying, inexpensive and easier than you would think to create your own. You can either use tesserae – small squares of mosaic glass, available from art and craft shops – as shown in the pictures here, or improvize with pieces of broken-up crockery, or even pebbles, shells and beads. The beauty of mosaic design is that it can be as small or large-scale as you like – the tiny mosaic fragments can even be used as shelf edgings – so you can adapt the size of your mosaic project to suit the time you have available. For a witty finishing touch, set off the real thing with mosaic-print fabrics.

◀ **Shimmering glass tesserae** in shades of copper, bronze and emerald are stuck side by side along the front edge of these shelves, defining their unusual curving lines. You can quickly and easily stick the tesserae in place using a glue gun.

▶ **Eye-catching blocks of mosaic** on the front of the work platform and around the corner window add colour, texture and a modern edge to this mellow-toned kitchen.

◢ **Cool blue**, perfectly square tesserae cover these bathroom walls and floor, giving a hardwearing, waterproof finish that's also the height of chic.

▼ **Simple but effective designs** are easy to create with tesserae tiles – like the symmetrical black and white pattern on this kitchen splashback. It's a good idea to work out your design on squared paper before you stick any tiles in place.

Index

ACKNOWLEDGEMENTS

Photographs

7 Abode UK, 8-9 Eaglemoss Publications/Steve Tanner, 10(t) Crown Paints, 10(b) Eaglemoss Publications/Steve Tanner, 11 IPC Magazines/Robert Harding Syndication, 12-13 Eaglemoss Publications/Martin Chaffer, 14 IPC Magazines/Robert Harding Syndication, 15 Eaglemoss Publications/Graham Rae, 16, 17 IPC Magazines/Robert Harding Syndication, 18(t) Mira Showers, 18(c,b) Eaglemoss Publications/Graham Rae, 19 Crown Paints, 20-21 Eaglemoss Publications/Steve Tanner, 22(t) EWA/Nadia McKenzie, 22(bl) Ikea, 22(br) IPC Magazines/Robert Harding Syndication, 23 EWA/Andreas von Einsiedel, 24-25, 26 Eaglemoss Publications/Steve Tanner, 27 EWA/Brian Harrison, 28-29 Eaglemoss Publications/Simon Page-Ritchie, 30(t) IPC Magazines/Robert Harding Syndication, 30(br) Eaglemoss Publications/Simon Page-Ritchie, 31 EWA/Andreas von Einsiedel, 32-33, 34 Eaglemoss Publications/Simon Page-Ritchie, 41-42 Eaglemoss Publications/Graham Rae, 45 English Stamp Company, 46, 47, 48(tl,tr) Eaglemoss Publications/Graham Rae, 48(bl) English Stamp Company, 48(br) DoehetZelf Holland, 49 IPC Magazines/Robert Harding Syndication, 50(tl) Elrose Products, 50 (bl) EWA/Shona Wood, 50(tr,cr,br) Woman & Home/PWA International, 51 Eaglemoss Publications/Adrian Taylor, 53 EWA/Spike Powell, 54 Eaglemoss Publications/Steve Tanner, 55 Eaglemoss Publications/Simon Page-Ritchie, 56(tr) EWA/Spike Powell, 56(cl) Sharps Bedrooms, 56(bl) Eaglemoss Publications/Simon Page-Ritchie, 56(br) IPC Magazines/Robert Harding Syndication, 57 LG Harris & Company, 58-59 EWA/Rodney Hyett, 60 EWA/Dennis Stone, 61 Eaglemoss Publications/Graham Rae, 62 Crown Paints, 63 IPC Magazines/Robert Harding Syndication, 64(t) EWA/Rodney Hyett, 64(bl)

Crown Paints, 64(bc,br) Eaglemoss Publications/Graham Rae, 65 Romo Fabrics, 67 Sanderson, 68 Eaglemoss Publications/Graham Rae, 69, 71 EWA/Andreas von Einsiedel, 72 Anna French, 74 Eaglemoss Publications/Iain Bagwell, 75 IPC Magazines/Robert Harding Syndication, 76-77(l) Eaglemoss Publications/Mark Wood, 77(br), 78(bl) Shand Kydd, 78(r) Eaglemoss Publications/Mark Wood, 79, 80(t,cl) Shand Kydd, 80(cr) IPC Magazines/Robert Harding Syndication, 80(b) Crown Wallcoverings, 81 Laura Ashley Home, 82(bl) Fablon, 82-83(t) Sanderson, 82-83(b) Laura Ashley Home, 84 Texas Homecare, 85 EWA/Andreas von Einsiedel, 86 IPC Magazines/Robert Harding Syndication, 87 EWA/Spike Powell, 88(t) Marie Claire IdÇes/Schwartz/Chastres/Lancrenon, 88(bl,br), 89 Eaglemoss Publications/Simon Page-Ritchie, 91, 92(t,bl) IPC Magazines/Robert Harding Syndication, 92(br) Abode UK, 93, 94(tl,tr) IPC Magazines/Robert Harding Syndication, 94(bl) EWA/Spike Powell, 94(br) Ariadne Holland, 95 Marie O'Hara, 96(tl,tr) IPC Magazines/Robert Harding Syndication, 96(bl) DoehetZelf Holland, 96(br) Paul Ryan, 97 IPC Magazines/Robert Harding Syndication, 98(tl) Sue Atkinson, 98(tr) Eaglemoss Publications/Martin Chaffer, 98(bl,br) Eaglemoss Publications/Simon Page-Ritchie, 99, 100(tl,bl) IPC Magazines/Robert Harding Syndication, 100(tr) Eaglemoss Publications/Mark Wood, 100(br) EWA/Nick Carter, 101 Eaglemoss Publications/Steve Tanner, 102(t) IPC Magazines/Robert Harding Syndication, 102(cl) EWA/Spike Powell, 102(cr) Eaglemoss Publications/Graham Rae, 102(b) Eaglemoss Publications/Simon Page-Ritchie, 103, 104(t,bl) IPC Magazines/Robert Harding Syndication, 104(br) EWA/David Giles, 105, 106(tl) Blue Hawk Ltd, 107(br) IPC Magazines/Robert Harding Syndication, 108(t) Vencel Resil, 108(b) Eaglemoss Publications/Simon Page-Ritchie, 109 IPC Magazines/Robert Harding Syndication, 110(t) EWA/Rodney Hyett, 110(b) World's End Tiles, 111(tl) Marlborough Tiles. 111(tr) Woman &

Home/PWA International, 111(b) Fired Earth, 112(tr) Eaglemoss Publications/Graham Rae, 112(bl) Brookman Kitchens, 112-113(b) Fired Earth, 113(t) Paul Ryan, 113(br) Stovax Ltd, 114(t) Fired Earth, 114(bl) Paul Ryan, 114(br) Eaglemoss Publications/Graham Rae, 115 H&R Johnson, 116-117(b) Osborne & Little, 117(tr) Fired Earth, 118 H&R Johnson, 119, 121 Eaglemoss Publications/Graham Rae, 122(bl) Fired Earth, 122-123(tr) Laura Ashley Home, 123(bl), 124(tr) Eaglemoss Publications/Graham Rae, 124(bl) IPC Magazines/Robert Harding Syndication, 125 Marie Claire Maison/Morel/Postic, 126(tl) IPC Magazines/Robert Harding Syndication, 126(tr,bl) EWA/Rodney Hyett, 126(br) EWA/Tom Leighton.

Illustrations

8-10 Sally Holmes, 12-14 Tig Sutton, 20 Sally Holmes, 24-26 Coral Mula, 28-30 Sally Holmes, 32-33 Coral Mula, 34 David Ashby, 35-36 Ian Sidaway, 37-38 Sally Holmes, 43-44 Ian Sidaway, 52 Sally Holmes, 54-56 Coral Mula, 58-60 Sally Holmes, 62-63 Coral Mula, 66-68 Tig Sutton, 70-72 Sally Holmes, 74 Coral Mula, 77-78 Sally Holmes, 82-84 Aziz Khan, 84(br) Stan North, 86-87 Sally Holmes, 89-90 David Ashby, 106-107 Coral Mula, 116-118, 120 Sally Holmes, 122-124 Tig Sutton.